A Credible Jesus
Fragments of a Vision

A Credible Jesus

Fragments of a Vision

ROBERT W. FUNK

Polebridge Press

A Credible Jesus: Fragments of a Vision

Published in 2002 by Polebridge Press, P. O. Box 6144, Santa Rosa, California, 95406.

ISBN 0-944344-88-7

Contents

Introduction
Voice Print

According to the evangelist Mark, people were astonished at Jesus' teaching, for he taught on his own authority, unlike the scholars.[1] This anecdote is undoubtedly a fiction created by Mark or some Christian storyteller who preceded him and from whom he borrowed the essence of the tale. Yet, to judge by his forms of speech and the impact he made upon his listeners, Jesus was unquestionably an orator of considerable rhetorical power. As Dominic Crossan puts it, "He was an illiterate peasant, but with an oral brilliance that few of those trained in literate and scribal disciplines can ever attain."[2]

Our purpose is not to praise Jesus, but to "place him" utilizing the subject matter of his speech and the modes of his public discourse. In order to locate him we must compare his language with ordinary modes of discourse in use in his time and place and in our own. After all, it will not be possible to understand what he was trying to tell his listeners if we do not comprehend his speech. The wisdom he attempted to communicate is embedded in his seemingly innocuous observations on the everyday world. What he is trying to say is the *tenor* of his discourse, which is something quite different from the apparent subject matter of his aphorisms and parables. The parable of the mustard seed, for example, is not about gardening. Indeed, the tenor of his words often seems unrelated to the literal sense of his words. To understand his vision, it will be necessary to observe how

1. Mark 1:22   2. *A Revolutionary Biography*, p. 58.

I

the two are intertwined. For it is his speech, in concert with his actions, that reveals how he viewed the world around him. And how he viewed the world around him supplies the constituent elements of his vision. And it is those elements – those startling insights – of which that we aspire to catch a glimpse.

By all accounts, Jesus was a wandering teacher of wisdom.

According to the gospels, his voice emanates from a repertoire of parables, aphorisms, and dialogues which the Jesus Seminar has isolated from the mass of tradition that accrued to his name. In those sayings and correlative acts we can occasionally catch sight of Jesus' vision of something he called God's domain.

Visions come in bits and pieces, in random stunning insights, never in continuous, articulated wholes. That is because visions are more than the sum of their parts. Yet from these fragments of insight we can begin to piece together some sense of the shape of the whole. To take an example, let's suppose that the following are authentic admonitions or pronouncements of the historical figure:

> love your enemies
> let the dead bury the dead
> turn the other cheek
> the domain of God belongs to the poor.

To what sort of flesh-and-blood person do they point? Approximately a hundred such fragments together provide us with glimpses of the historical figure, or least the way he saw the world. Since his vision is made up of a constellation of glimpses, the best we can hope for is a glimpse of few facets of his vision. Our glimpse will be a glimpse of his glimpse.

The body of this book consists of seventeen short essays based on aphorisms, parables, dialogues, and deeds. Each cameo is a fragment of Jesus' vision. Together they project the contours of the whole. We cannot, of course, fill in all the detail, but we can catch sight of the historical figure here and there, now and then, in these tiny windows that open onto his words and work.

A single face in a Galilean crowd

The process of constructing, or reconstructing, a profile of the historical figure can be no more successful than identifying and isolating his real words and actual acts. To be sure, imagination is then required to piece together the fragments of his vision into something like a continuous whole. To succeed in this task, we must be prepared to observe what Jesus typically talked about; and we must ask how he talked about it, since the mode of discourse is as important as the subject matter. Even then we are only at the threshold of his perceptions of the world about him. We must next ask what kind of knowledge he attempted to communicate. To ascend to that height it is essential to combine subject matter, mode of discourse, and kind of knowledge into one seamless fabric. That is the final challenge. Of course, we will have to go on and ask whether his deeds, in so far as we can recover them from the stories told about him, match his words. Assuming that the two are reasonably congruent, we might then have captured at least a silhouette of the historical figure.

It is sometimes assumed that extensive historical knowledge of the period, especially of Judaism as it was practiced in Galilee, is essential to profiling Jesus. That assumption rests on another: Jesus was like most other Jews living in Galilee at the time. On that view, all we need to do is to adjust our portrait of Jesus to that general picture and we have the historical figure. Unfortunately, that is not good history, for the "typical Jew" of Galilee in Jesus' day is made up of stereotypes that represent no particular individuals. Although Jesus was certainly a Jew, we cannot identify his particular face if we are unable to distinguish it from other Jewish (and gentile) faces in a Galilean crowd.

Christian scholars have been inclined to the opposite assumption, namely, that Jesus is pretty much as he is represented in the New Testament gospels. He is, so to speak, a "Christian," in practice if not in title. His early followers understood him well, we are led to suppose, and their knowledge is embodied in the four gospels. Again, that is patently inaccurate. We now know that the

New Testament gospels are theological from beginning to end. They focus not so much on Jesus the man and teacher as Jesus the son of man or son of God, and they allow their portraits to be deeply influenced by that assumption. Critical scholars are agreed that the historical figure differs in numerous important respects from the picture painted of him in the four canonical stories.

These twin problems present us with a delicate task. On the one hand, we must distinguish Jesus from typical forms of Judaism, without however separating him from his ethnic heritage. If he said and did nothing distinctive, how can we hope to create a historical profile? In that case, the story of any contemporary Jew would suffice. But we have dozens of portraits of contemporary Jews, and those portraits differ in myriad ways from one another. So we are obliged to locate a Jew, but a Jew with a difference. That should not be difficult given the richness and depth of the Jewish tradition represented by the Torah, the great prophets, the wisdom tradition, and rabbinic lore.

On the other hand, we cannot allow that Christian representations of Jesus are all historically correct. Doubtless in the stories told about him and the words ascribed to him there are memory traces of the historical figure. But in which of those acts and words are they to be found? Since we cannot assume Jesus was a "Christian" as that term was understood in the eighties and nineties of the first century when Matthew and Luke were composing their gospels, we must also contrast him with that portrait. His admirers turned Jesus the iconoclast into Jesus the icon. They exchanged his view of God's domain for their vision of him.

We are caught between the Scylla of a stereotyped first-century Judaism and the Charybdis of Christian propaganda. To navigate those treacherous waters requires considerable skill. We can do no better than say how we intend to proceed and allow the reader to judge for herself or himself how well we succeed.

Entry point: The words of Jesus

We begin with the words attributed to Jesus. We do so because in the case of words we are dealing with something that was repeated. The ancient gospels are filled with sentences that begin, "Jesus said," . . . followed by words attributed to him. With a few minor exceptions, all the words ascribed to Jesus are preserved in Greek. It is all but certain, however, that his native tongue was Aramaic. If he could not speak Greek, then we will never be able to recover a significant number of his actual words. Yet since the early Jesus movement consistently represents him as speaking Greek, some scholars have concluded that he was bilingual. Although Jesus was probably technically illiterate, many Jews in the first century were literate in Greek. Some wrote extensively in Greek. Indeed, among the works that can be attributed to Jewish authors in that period, more than half were composed originally in Greek. Others were translated from Hebrew or Aramaic into Greek. Even the leaders of the second Jewish revolt wrote letters to each other in Greek. We have some reason, then, to believe the formation of the Jesus tradition took place in Greek. That does not mean that we have the actual words of Jesus. What we have are memories of the gist of what he said, and in some instances a fair representation of how he said it.

In the case of stories about what Jesus did, on the other hand, we are dealing with third person reports or accounts of what he is remembered to have done. Jesus did not tell stories about himself. He is never represented as saying something like, "I remember the day I went up to Jerusalem to visit the temple, . . . " or "I recall when my mother said to me, 'Jesus, . . . '" Jesus seems not to have talked much about himself. When he does so in the gospels, it is probably the community having Jesus speak its convictions about him, rather than Jesus himself speaking.

Just as we do not have first person accounts from the lips of Jesus, we do not have eyewitness reports about the events that occurred during his lifetime. For example, there are three stories about the conversion of the first disciples. They do not agree in either location or personnel. Obviously someone other than the actual participants is relating the story. Had these stories been formulated by actual participants, they would have a higher level of consistency and plausibility. The stories we have in the gospels are anecdotes created and circulated orally for decades before they were finally written down. Even then there was preference for the oral form, which was taken to be more authentic than the written. After all, writing fixes the tradition, while oral reports are living language. In an oral culture, scribes were looked upon with considerable skepticism. Just consult the scorn heaped on scribes in the gospels.

So we begin with the words.

Aphorisms and parables

Jesus is remembered as a sage whose dominant forms of public speech included the aphorism, the parable, and the dialogue. We begin by collecting those speech forms (the database we shall employ is catalogued in Appendix 3) and analyzing them for style and content. Let us begin with the speech forms.

The Aphorism

Jesus was a master of the short, pithy witticism known as an aphorism. We need to distinguish an aphorism from a proverb.

A proverb expresses conventional wisdom. It affirms what everybody already knows or suspects. It is default wisdom – the wisdom we revert to when we are not thinking about things or confronting situations for which we do not have a prescription. "An apple a day keeps the doctor away" is a typical proverb. *Poor Richard's Almanac*, assembled by Dr. Benjamin Franklin, is loaded with traditional wisdom, much of which is still in active circulation. "God helps those who help themselves," "haste makes waste," and "no pain, no gain," are found in that collection. There are less well known proverbs that are quite good: I like "Little boats must keep near the shore" and "Little strokes fell great oaks." These are received or proverbial wisdom at their best. (I use "received" in the sense of wisdom that has been accepted as true and authoritative because it is part of a common heritage.)

In contrast, an aphorism subverts or contradicts conventional proverbial wisdom. "Let the dead bury the dead" is one of Jesus' most difficult aphorisms.[3] "Let the dead bury the dead" attacks the fundamental obligation to care appropriately for the dead, and it does so by suggesting that many living are metaphorically dead.

"Don't let your left hand in on what your right hand is up to" is a paradox.[4] It is a demand impossible of fulfillment, yet it prompts modesty in acts of charity, which is what its context in Matthew suggests.

"It is easier for a camel to squeeze through the eye of a needle than for a person of wealth to gain entrance to God's domain."[5] This aphorism is hyperbole: it says something about the dimensions of the door to God's domain, but it does so metaphorically rather than literally. A number of Jesus' aphorisms suggest that we cannot, indeed we must not, take them entirely literally.

Oscar Wilde was a well-known modern aphorist. One of his best is, "We wouldn't be so concerned about what people thought of us, if we realized how seldom they do." We laugh because it catches us with our guard down: we do worry about what people think of us when that worry may be entirely misplaced.

Flannery O'Connor was asked repeatedly whether she thinks universities stifle writers. Her response, "Probably, but they don't stifle nearly enough of them."

Halford Luccock, who taught homiletics at Yale University for many years, was once asked, "How many points should a sermon have?" "At least one," he replied. Like that of Flannery O'Connor, Luccock's aphorism is the climax of a dialogue, and it functions as an aphorism only in that context.

These are examples of the short, memorable statement that subverts our expectations. We remember them precisely because they contradict what we normally think.

3. Matt 8:22   4. Matt 6:3   5. Matt 19:24

The Parable

The parable is the other dominant form of Jesus' wisdom. The parable is a fiction – a made-up story about things and events in the everyday world. In Jesus' repertoire there are full narrative parables consisting of two scenes and at least three characters, along with abbreviated parables having only one participant.

The foreground of the parable consists of commonplaces, concrete events and things. Jesus distorts or parodies those commonplaces by hyperbole, metaphor, caricature, ambiguity, or paradox. Having begun with typifications, he then detypifies by distorting or parodying the everyday world. In the process, Jesus turns the story or picture into a fantasy, a fantasy about God's domain, an order of reality that derives from but subtly transforms the everyday world. It is about an order of reality that lies beyond, but just barely beyond, the everyday, the humdrum, the habituated. Because the parable sets the ordinary in a new frame of reference, the parable is also an invitation to cross over, to leave the old behind and embrace the new.

In the parable of the vineyard laborers, for example, Jesus depicts an ordinary scene: The owner of a vineyard goes into the village square to hire workers to harvest his grapes.[6] He does so repeatedly during the day, including one trip just an hour before the day ends. Jesus thus literalizes and then caricatures the hiring process. Because he does so, we as listeners are led to anticipate a surprising ending. And we are not disappointed: the owner pays all the workers the same wage, those who worked the twelve-hour shift along with those who toiled only an hour. Jesus does not tell us why the proprietor does that. Jesus does not tell us what the parable means. We must figure that out for ourselves. But it is clear that the story subverts the normal system of employment and wages. The parables thus appear to hint at a counter reality, a different scheme of things that contrasts with the conventional, the established order.

The parables proved to be difficult to imitate. Parables are not

6. Matt 20:1–15

attributed to anyone else in the gospel tradition. They appear only in the synoptic gospels; John contains none at all. Aphorisms, on the other hand, were common in the hellenistic world, so the Jesus repertoire grows exponentially in proverbial lore as it matures. The line between aphorism and proverb, accordingly, became less and less distinct as time went by.

Dialogues, in so far as they represent actual exchanges Jesus may have had with others, usually climax in an aphorism or a parable. In some cases, the dialogue may have been an invented context for some saying of Jesus. In a few cases, there may be actual memories of exchanges Jesus had with disciples or critics.

Rhetorical strategies

Jesus develops a consistent rhetorical strategy that involves what he said, how he said it (or did it), and what he meant by it. In other words, his strategy matches the content of his message. That strategy and its consequences may be sketched in the following categories.

Jesus inhabits the same everyday world that he shares with his Galilean contemporaries. He may see that world differently than many of his contemporaries, but he certainly shares a common world with them. We can discover both the world he shares and how he differs from other perceptions of it by reading his stories and witticisms closely. Reading Deuteronomy, or the Talmud, or Josephus, or Philo won't tell us who Jesus is. They will help establish the received reality sense, but the world Jesus knew and lived in is revealed through his figures of speech and stories. That world was was *his* world, a world he shared with his contemporaries. He learned it from his mother and father, from his Nazareth neighbors, from traveling philosophers he may have encountered in Sepphoris, or from an occasional text he may have come across if he were able to read. It might be superfluous to make the mundane point that Jesus' world can be determined only by his words and deeds, except that historians and biblical interpreters tend to forget it in their haste to exhibit their knowledge. When writing for an academic audience, we cite many texts and the judgments of our colleagues as to what Jesus thought — as though the Qumran scrolls or a learned analysis of the letters of Ignatius or even the author of the Fourth Gospel is a better guide to what Jesus perceived than the evidence provided by what he himself says and does.

The index to his lived world are his sayings and the anecdotes that portray him acting on his own pronouncements. These are the essential clues to his disposition to things, to his perceptions of the scene about him, and to his view of his tradition. All the rest has to be judged by reference to the direct sight and insights provided by those clues. And his lived world has to be distinguished from the received or default world that predominates in his society. That world, too, can be inferred from the typifications with which he begins.

We begin with the revealing observation that his language is concrete and specific. Jesus always talked about God's domain in everyday, mundane terms. He talks about a woman baking bread, he speaks of dinner parties, of day laborers sitting on their haunches waiting to be hired, of a manager who embezzles funds from his employer, of camels passing through a gate, of a den of foxes, of birds and flowers.

He never uses abstract language. He does not make philosophical generalizations. He would not have said, "I think; therefore I am." He would not have observed that homo sapiens is the only animal that has language. He made no theological statements. He would not have said, "I believe in God the Father Almighty," or "All human beings have sinned and fallen short of the glory of God." It would never even have occurred to him to assert that "God is love." If he thought God were love, he would have told a story to that effect. But God would not have been a character in the story. He rarely talks about God directly. Jesus did not have a doctrine of God; he seems to have had some experience of God.

The varied foci of Jesus' sayings provides an informative list. These are the topics of his discourse:

a woman baking bread
wild mustard growing in a garden
a storage jar with a broken handle
the victim of a mugging on a lonely road
day laborers sitting around on their haunches waiting to be
hired
a recalcitrant son who emigrates to a foreign country
a dinner party
a manager who embezzles funds from his employer
a slave who cannot forgive a minor debt
the loss of a coin on the dirt floor of a house
a stray sheep
a cache of coins discovered in a field
an exquisite pearl
two men at prayer in the temple area
unscrupulous judges
an assassin practicing with his sword
poverty stricken peasants
camels passing by
anxieties about food and clothing
flowers in the field
birds in the sky
hungry beggars at the city gate
a man being sued for a garment given in pledge
a den of foxes
a wedding feast
someone washing dishes
the death of a father
a family enclave
a beggar with dermatitis
walking through grainfields on the sabbath
tribal enemies
people taking each other to court
homeless, demon-possessed people without caretakers
bankers making loans at usurious rates
the demand for taxes

displays of public piety
the commercialization of the temple
a Roman soldier conscripting a peasant's assistance
the practice of hospitality to strangers
rejection by friends and neighbors in one's hometown
a friend pounding on the door at midnight

These and similar topics are the focal points of Jesus' picture of the world; they constitute the ostensible subject matter of his parables and witticisms. As he looked about him, these are things on which he fastened. This very fact bespeaks the nature of his vision: how he perceived the ordinary reality of his friends and neighbors in contrast to his vision of God's domain, the alternative reality he sought to establish. Jesus' vision did not have to do with lofty theories or grand abstractions. It did not derive from the interpretation of ancient texts. With very few exceptions, Jesus does not appeal to the priesthood, or the temple, or purity distinctions, to the scribes, or to the Torah.

Jesus' concrete and specific language depicts the horizon of his everyday world, the world he shares with his Galilean neighbors. That language employs typifications. In his parables and aphorisms, Jesus makes use of typifications to which everyone in his audience could have given immediate assent. A manager embezzles from his employer. A woman loses a coin on the dirt floor of her house. A judge is corrupt. A friend knocks on the door at midnight and asks for bread. A truant son asks for his inheritance and then blows it on wine, women, and song in a foreign land. Listeners nod their heads in agreement with these overstated generalizations. His exaggerations call attention to those aspects of life the average person thinks of as "typical."

He epitomizes his sense of the world by bringing to attention aspects that match ordinary perceptions. In the Samaritan, someone gets mugged, robbed, and left for dead on the Roman road to Jericho (still a common occurrence we are told two thousand years later on a tour in Israel). Two men go up to the temple to pray. Jesus is surrounded by peasants who are poverty stricken. People make public displays of piety in the form of prayer and alms. The government demands taxes. The poor are anxious about what they will eat and wear. These are all represented as ordinary events in Jesus' world.

The human default world is the sum of typifications. Language is the house of typifications. In our politically correct society, typifications are scorned. Individuals like to think they are different in most important respects. But that is not the case. Our society is given to patterns of behavior, eating, dressing, working. Franchised restaurants, shopping malls, and churches with steeples betray a shared reality.

Basic typifications are conceived in the face-to-face situation. Then they become increasingly crystallized as they lose sight of the particular, the exception, with reference to which they were conceived. To say that priests and levites are uncaring is to speak anonymously of most priests, as though the rare exception were the rule. To assert that the pious are pompous is a generalization representative of no one in particular. People are always taking each other to court – or so it seems. Because Jesus was a social deviant, he concludes he cannot not be honored by hometown folks. That is not necessarily true either, although the proverb will have it so. Because these are typifications, which do not apply to every case, we cannot take them literally. But they are a provocative point of departure for Jesus' call to renounce what is typical in favor of his vision of God's domain where everything is exceptional. Jesus then distorts and dismantles the everyday world by indulging in metaphor, hyperbole, caricature, reversals, ambiguity, paradox, and parody. We know his language is not literal because his rhetoric resists such an interpretation. Hyperbole, reversals, and conflict between fact and metaphor clearly undermine the literal.

Although his language was drawn from the mundane world around him, he did not have ordinary reality in mind. His language is indirect; it is highly figurative or metaphorical. We know the parable of the leaven is not about baking bread. The dinner party has nothing to do with social etiquette or with seating patterns at a banquet. The mustard seed and the sower are not about gardening. The shrewd manager does not offer advice about business practices. His admonition to lend to those who can't pay us back is not about banking practice. While he speaks unceasingly in mundane terms, about what appears to be trivial or trite matters, his listeners know he has some other, much more significant subject in mind.

Jesus' exaggerations, his caricatures, his parodies point to the real subject matter of his discourse, the reign of God. These rhetorical ploys do not permit the listener to take his stories, his metaphors, at face value.

Three people are invited to a dinner party; they refuse at the last moment to come; hundreds from the street are then herded into the hall. The discrepancy is fantastic.

A slave has a debt of ten million dollars cancelled, but he is unable to forgive a debt of ten dollars. The contrast is ludicrous.

He frustrates ordinary expectations, moreover, by reversing what we anticipate will be the case. In the parable of the vineyard laborers, those who work only one hour are paid the same wage as those who labored the entire day. We do not think that is fair; it contradicts our concept of logic.

In the parable of the prodigal, the truant son is welcomed home like royalty, when we think he should have been reprimanded and chastised.

When Jesus proclaims, "Congratulations, you hungry! You'll have a feast," he is turning all ordinary expectations around.[7] In many such passages, Jesus is a humorist, like Mark Twain or Will Rogers. He makes free use of parody. The parable of the empty jar in the Gospel of Thomas pokes fun at the story of the jar of meal miraculously replenished by Elijah for the widow of Zarepath. The Mustard Seed ridicules the image of the mighty cedar of Lebanon employed by Ezekiel as a symbol for the mighty kingdom of David.

Jesus indulges in other forms of humor. In the parable of the lost coin, the woman spends the value of the coin she has just recovered in celebrating her good fortune. The shepherd recovers the lost sheep and promptly announces a celebration, which

7. Luke 6:20

probably involved the slaughter of a sheep. Jesus' listeners must have laughed at these hidden travesties on sober speech.

We can think of Jesus as the first standup Jewish comic; he can properly be described as a comic savant – a sage who embeds wisdom in humor; a humorist who shuns practical advice. "If someone sues you for your coat, give him the shirt off your back to go with it." That is not practical advice: to follow it is to go naked.[8] Comic wisdom refuses to be explicit. Yet in the stories he tells, the sage constructs a new fiction that becomes the basis for his or her own action and the action of others. The contours of that fiction are ambiguous in order to frustrate moralizing proclivities; they are also open to multiple and deeper interpretations as a way of keeping them open to reinterpretation in ever new contexts. Our task is to follow their lead and figure out what meaning to give them in our own circumstances.

He often combines the literal and the figurative in order to create tension. "Give to everyone who begs from you" is an example.[9] His listeners knew they should practice acts of charity, but how could they respond positively to every request without financial ruin? Here he combines the typical with the metaphorical to create his point.

Jesus was plied with questions, to which he never gave direct answers. "Should we pay taxes?" he was asked. His ambiguous but not evasive response was, "Pay the emperor what belongs to the emperor and pay God what belongs to God."[10]

By employing these rhetorical tactics, he infringes the existing paradigm and initiates a new reality. His words are a door to that alternative reality. Jesus adopts that new reality sense as his own, so far as we can tell. It becomes *his* default reality, which he attempts to share with his followers through his words and deeds.

This way of speaking about the kingdom of God is necessary because God's domain is not immediately observable. He employs tropes or figures of speech drawn from the sensible world to speak obliquely or indirectly, and therefore metaphorically, about another realm. His followers remember him warning

8. Matt 5:40
9. Matt 5:42a
10. Mark 12:17

them repeatedly, "Those here with two good ears had better listen."[11] What he was trying to convey was subtle and covert. He was undermining the immense solidity of the received world with a vision of an alternative reality. His words communicate in a non-ordinary sense. The knowledge he communicates is pre-conceptual, the experience of reality unsegmented, of an undifferentiated nexus, of a seamless universe of meaning. His parables and aphorisms embody a world coming into being. When combined, the hundreds of observations he makes on events in the everyday world form a vision of some new reality, quite unlike the habituated world.

Some of his followers got the idea right away. They began to see and act on his vision. But they had difficulty interpreting it for themselves in new situations, and transmitting it to others because it was not prescriptive, codified. It was non-literal. They were puzzled by the irony, paradox, parody, and metaphor. So they converted his insights into things they found more useful: They took his basic insights and adopted tables of received virtue and baptized those virtues as their own. They developed sanctions to enforce those virtues and views. They did so on his authority, now believed to be that of a teacher sent from God. An orthodoxy emerged. By the fourth century, the church's salvation machine was in place. Now converts had to submit to the beliefs and practices of the institution in order to merit salvation. Dissidents were deemed heretics. There was no salvation outside the church. And the kingdom had now been transferred to another world, the world beyond the grave and beyond history. Nevertheless, here and there in the tradition one can catch a glimpse of the original – the powerful poet who broke out of the mold and mounted a challenge to the world. And some still get it, in spite of the obfuscating debris of the orthodox tradition preserved in the New Testament gospels and the creeds.

How was Jesus himself related to his vision? We cannot write a biography of Jesus' life; the data are insufficient. We cannot infer much about his interior life. But we can draw some conclusions about him from his way of speaking about God's domain.

11. Mark 4:9

Jesus speaks and acts on his own authority, on the authority of his vision. He does not quote sources. Unlike other teachers, he does not cite and interpret scripture. He does not footnote his assertions with references to other sages. He does not debate fine points in the law. He is not a scribe, a scholar, by disposition. He is an oral sage, who articulates a vision first of all for himself. He is his own authority in that new world.

And he derives his own identity from that same vision. He is who he is by virtue of the world he now inhabits. He cannot be self-referential because his vision has captured him, not the other way around. He tells his parables as though he were hearing them, and he articulates his witty insights as realities to which he gives himself.

Consequently, he does not make personal confessions. He does not refer to himself as the son of man or the son of God. He does not think of himself as the messiah. It is inconceivable that he said, "I am the way, the truth, and the life; no one comes to the Father except through me." On the contrary, his discourse is focused exclusively on the banalities of the everyday world as they are transformed in God's realm.

We must now consider these banalities as hints about his vision of God's domain. We will do so in a series of chapters, each of which is a fragment of his vision. Although it is risky to do so, we might locate them on a general map to guide the reader in her or his journey.

The first three chapters, *The Invisible Realm, A Trust Ethic,* and *Celebration,* present glimpses of the primary aspects of Jesus' vision. These aspects function as the foundation on which other glimpses rest.

The next set of chapters sketches out the scope of God's domain. *Outsiders & Outcasts* indicates how social boundaries are broken down within Jesus' society; *Transcending Tribalism* shows how his vision exceeds the limits of the tribe; *Kinship* registers how Jesus attempted to break out of the prison of the patriarchal family structure; and finally, *Flora and Fauna* gathers Jesus' perspectives on the world of nature.

Chapters eight through thirteen illustrate how Jesus' vision subverts the everyday world. *Values Are Counterintuitive;* Jesus introduces new symbols that parody traditional symbols; behavior in God's domain subverts the social and economic system in place. In Jesus' vision, the world has been swept clean of demonic powers. For Jesus rewards under God's rule are intrinsic; no further reward us expected or desired. Finally, traces of humor and humility in Jesus' rhetoric indicate that he was no moralist. All of these features are facets of the reign of God as subversive of default reality.

It seems clear that Jesus had little use for the temple cult. For him persons had direct access to God without benefit of priest or sacrifice. God did not require brokers. The Jesus movement forgot that basic dictum early on in its development.

Three final chapters read across the aphorisms, parables, and anecdotes. In *The Unkingdom of the UnGod*, we have collected evidence that Jesus employs the language of God as king ironically: for him it contravenes the traditional way of representing God as a royal monarch. It follows from this notion that the domain of God must be a mythic destination: we can see it from afar, but we can never reach it. There will always be some new desert to cross, some new enemy to love, some new default reality to replace with a fresh vision. The last chapter is an effort to salvage the symbol of the cross by interpreting it as a symbol of absolute integrity, of the refusal to compromise. It is doubtful that we can overturn the orthodox interpretation of Jesus' death as an atoning death by understanding it in the context of what he said and did, but it is worth a try.

The conclusion attempts to draw these glimpses together in an integrated whole. The primary figure is Jesus' use of the narrow door as a metaphor of the difficulty attending any effort to enter God's domain. The narrow door opens onto an alternative reality, which Jesus takes to be more real than the merely ordinary but nevertheless located right there in the everyday. His glimpses catch sight of the extraordinary in the ordinary.

The
Invisible
Realm

Coming of God's Imperial Rule (1)

His disciples said to him, "When will the Father's imperial rule come?"

[2]"It will not come by watching for it. [3]It will not be said, 'Look, here!' or 'Look, there!' [4]Rather, the Father's imperial rule is spread out upon the earth, and people don't see it."

Sources: Q, Thomas • Thom 113:1–4

Coming of God's Imperial Rule (2)

When asked by the Pharisees when God's imperial rule would come, he answered them, "You won't be able to observe the coming of God's imperial rule. People are not going to be able to say, 'Look, here it is!' or 'Over there!' On the contrary, God's imperial rule is right there in your presence."

Sources: Q, Thomas • Luke 17:20–21

Award to the Poor

Congratulations, you poor! God's domain belongs to you.

Source: Q • Luke 6:20

Eye of a Needle

It's easier for a camel to squeeze through a needle's eye, than for a wealthy person to get into God's domain.

Source: Mark • Matt 19:24

Difficult for Wealthy

How difficult it is for those who have money to enter God's domain.

Source: Mark • Mark 10:23

Rich Farmer

There was a rich person who had a great deal of money. [2]He said, "I shall invest my money so that I may sow, reap, plant, and fill my storehouses with produce, that I may lack nothing." [3]These were the things he was thinking in his heart, but that very night he died.

Sources: Thomas, Luke • Thom 63:1–3

Two Masters

No one can be a slave to two masters. No doubt that slave will either hate one and love the other, or be devoted to one and disdain the other. You can't be enslaved to both God and a bank account.

Sources: Q, Thomas • Matt 6:24

The Invisible Realm

Terminology

The theme of Jesus' public discourse was the *basileia tou theou* (pronounced *ba-si-lá-ya toú the-oú)*, traditionally translated the kingdom of God, to use the language of the King James Bible. The *Basileus (ba-si-loús)* is the ruler, the emperor, the king, the queen, the monarch, the tyrant, the head of the state. And the state was the realm or reach of that dominion. Kingdom language was in vogue in the seventeenth century at the time the King James Bible was created, as it was in the ancient Near East. It is no longer in vogue to the same extent, in part because royalty has lost its appeal for modern democracies, and in part because it strikes many as sexist language. (We never seem to refer to the royal state as the "queendom," but we do speak of the animal kingdom.)

In the Scholars Version, we have translated the phrase as God's domain or God's imperial rule, using the first when a place is intended, and the second when a process appears to be the reference. To the poor, Jesus promises that God's domain or realm belongs to them. When the talk is of "God's imperial rule closing in," the reference is to the process or act.

"Kingdom" is an archaic metaphor (from the modern point of view) for the region or sphere where God's dominion is immediate and absolute. In fact, we considered the phrase "empire of God" on the grounds that the words in Greek would have called the "Roman Empire" to mind. In any case, God's domain pits the sovereignty of God against the power of whatever political empire was then in place. The loci of power in that society were, first of all, the state, followed by the town or city, and then the extended family. So Jesus is reported to have said that every "government" *(basileia)* divided against itself is devastated, and every household (the extended family) at odds with itself will fall. In one version of this saying, the town is inserted between state and family. These terms provide an overview of the social organization of Jesus' world.

We shall suggest later that Jesus employed the royal designation ironically: When taken literally, it recalls the glorious days of King David and his kingdom, but the realm of God as Jesus conceives it contrasts sharply with the dominant features of the Davidic kingdom – its power and wealth and success. For Jesus, God's realm contrasts with the Davidic notion of kingdom and those contrasting features are expressed in a variety of aphorisms. The term *kingdom* is thus not appropriate as a designation for the domain or dominion of God.

In this chapter, we will explore two sets of aphorisms related to the contrast between the Davidic kingdom and God's realm. The first indicates that the domain of God is an invisible realm. The second asserts that it is peopled with those who have been marginalized in society. However, all the features that emerge from the profile of Jesus support the basic notion that God's realm is hidden.

God's dominion is everywhere present but not demonstrable

The domain of God is not visible to those bound by traditional notions of power and authority. Jesus believed God's reign to be present, but not discernible to lazy or sleepy eyes, or eyes conditioned by the received world. The domain of God was an invisible realm; most people, whether naïve or sophisticated, are oblivious to God's rule, as is indicated by this saying:

His disciples said to him, "When will the Father's imperial rule come?"

"It will not come by watching for it. It will not be said, 'Look, here!' or 'Look, there!' Rather, the Father's imperial rule is spread out upon the earth, and people don't see it."[1]

1. Thom 113:1–4

It is evident that this saying is related to one found in the Gospel of Luke:

> When asked by the Pharisees when God's imperial rule would come, he answered them, "You won't be able to observe the coming of God's imperial rule. People are not going to be able to say, 'Look, here it is!' or 'Over there!' On the contrary, God's imperial rule is right there in your presence."[2]

Since Luke and Thomas are independent sources, the saying is older than either of them.

These two synoptic siblings, as Steve Patterson terms them,[3] pose interesting questions. First, this form of remark about the coming of God's imperial rule appears atypical of Jesus' style. Here he speaks about God's domain directly but negatively; elsewhere he refers to that realm only indirectly, by analogy, but positively. The Domain of God, he suggests, is like a mustard seed[4] or like leaven.[5] Jesus may speak of those to whom God's domain belongs (the poor) or does not belong (the rich), or the expulsion of demons may announce the arrival of God's imperial rule.[6] But otherwise Jesus rarely speaks of God's presence in its own right, without a metaphor or analogy. The reign of God is not normally visible, according to Jesus; it cannot be observed by just anybody. By the conventional standards of the everyday world, the default world, the divine domain is simply invisible. It is a hidden or secret realm.

The fact that God's imperial rule is customarily hidden from human eyes explains why one cannot say, "Look, here it is!" or "Look, over there!" Luke does not quite follow through in drawing out the implications of this warning the way Thomas does. In Thomas, the evidence of God's rule is everywhere, but people just don't see it. It is hidden from them. Luke's phrase, "God's domain is among you," which the Scholars Version has translated, "is right there in your presence," is ambiguous.

2. Luke 17:20

3. *Thomas and Jesus*, 71–72.

4. Luke 13:18//Matt 17:31

5. Luke 13:20//Matt 13:33

6. Luke 11:20

The tradition struggled with the paradox. On the one hand, Jesus' followers wanted to be assertive in proclaiming the presence of God's reign. On the other, they were constrained by the apocalyptic view they had inherited from John the Baptist that God's reign was a future event. The two views are combined in the sequence put together by Luke in 17:20–21 (cited above) followed by vv. 22–25. Luke announces the presence of God's reign in v. 21 and then depicts a distant future event when God's rule will really arrive.

> And he said to the disciples, "There'll come a time when you will yearn to see one of the days of the son of Adam, and you won't see it. And they'll be telling you, `Look, there it is!' or 'Look, here it is!' Don't rush off; don't pursue it. For just as lightning flashes and lights up the sky from one end to the other, that's what the son of Adam will be like in his day.[7]

Luke doesn't object to the eventual apocalyptic coming of the God's reign, but he rejects an imminent apocalyptic event. Accordingly, he warns: "And they'll be telling you, 'Look, there it is!' or 'Look, here it is!' Don't rush off; don't pursue it." The clichés 'Look, there it is!' or 'Look, here it is!' appear in a variety of contexts that have to do with false signs and portents that deceive and lead astray. The popular Christian tradition has never been able to resist the temptation to look for signs and portents that herald the presence of the messiah or the arrival of the kingdom. Apocalypticism too soon succumbs to the temptation to assemble a list of supernatural markers. Even Matthew, who is by no means adverse to the apocalyptic view, has gathered the warnings against such speculation in this passage:

> Then if someone says to you, "Look, here is the Anointed" or "over here," don't count on it! After all, counterfeit messiahs and phony prophets will show up, and they'll offer great portents and miracles to delude, if possible, even the chosen people. Look, I have warned you in advance. In fact, if they should say to you, "Look, he's in the wilderness," don't go

---

7. Luke 17:22–24

out there; "Look, he's in one of the secret rooms," don't count on it. For just as lightning comes out of the east and is visible all the way to the west, that's what the coming of the son of Adam will be like. For wherever there's a corpse, that's where vultures gather.[8]

In particular the evangelist warns against locating the presence of God in some specific locality, such as the wilderness (the haven of apocalyptic groups in the first century as in the twentieth) or in secret chambers (secret societies). The final aphorism, "Wherever there's a corpse, that's where the vultures gather," is an apt commentary on the character of those who trade in the "Look, there, look, here" syndrome and indulge in such idle speculation.

What does it mean to say that God's rule is in your presence, or spread out on the earth though people do not see it?

The saying is a strong affirmation that God's imperial rule is everywhere present. God is really in charge of the universe, even though the divine presence is not evident. The reason there is no need for prognostication as in the case of apocalyptic expectations is that God's domain is everywhere. But of course it remains unobserved because it contravenes the normal reality code. The surface evidence is against it.

Scholars have labored mightily to account for Luke's ambiguous phrase. Some modern interpreters have been inclined to understand "among you" as "in you," which suggests something internal to the human psyche, some inward power. That appeals to modern individualism, but is certainly not the original sense. The problem is that the kingdom is nowhere depicted as a property of the heart or the private self. It is always something public, something obvious to the eyes of faith. A second group of interpreters has taken the phrase to refer to the presence of Jesus as the messiah among the Galileans. The phrase would then be an oblique self-reference. A third group has suggested that the phrase means "within your reach or grasp." Of these possibilities, only the third approximates Jesus' meaning.

8. Matt 24:23–28

When we interpret the sayings of Jesus, most of which were transmitted without context, we must make use of other authentic sayings to understand them. We are obliged to form a profile of Jesus from a compendium of sayings, the individual items of which are used to interpret each other. And in this case, the best resort is to other sayings that bear on the meaning of God's domain in your presence. The possibility that Jesus uttered a saying in which he asserts that God's reign is present but invisible is confirmed by other features of God's imperial rule as he envisions them.

A domain of nobodies

The first beatitude is powerful evidence for the secret or hidden nature of God's dominion.

Congratulations, you poor! God's domain belongs to you!

In Jesus' world, the poor and destitute were quite visible. He is probably congratulating the poverty stricken standing around him. They were being awarded something they did not know they possessed. It probably surprised them. They may even have tittered or laughed aloud at the preposterous suggestion that the poor were favorites of God. There is no empirical warrant for the assertion that the poor are blessed. The only warrant is their alleged status in the invisible kingdom of Jesus.

The traditional view was that success in the economic and political world followed upon the correct observation of the covenant and the purity codes. The covenantal blessings and curses are outlined in Deuteronomy 28.

> When you have crossed the Jordan and entered the land the Lord your God gives you, if you pay attention to the voice of the Lord your God and guard and observe all the commandments I, Moses, give you this day, you may depend on it, the Lord your God will assign you a place exalted high above all

the nations of the earth. All these blessings will be yours if you listen carefully to the voice of the Lord your God.[9]

There then follows in Deut 28:3–14 a list of the blessings that Israel will enjoy provided she keeps the commandments. Included among them is the promise that Israel will lend to many nations but will not have to borrow from them. However, if the people and their rulers do not observe the codes, they will be cursed.

> Similarly, you may depend on it, if you do not obey the voice of the Lord your God and guard and keep all the commandments that I have given you this day, the following calamities will befall you.[10]

There then follows a list of calamities that Israel may expect, an unmitigated list of disasters.[11]

This paradigm is applied throughout the deuteronomic history that extends from the book of Joshua through 2 Kings. Jesus seems to have been in fundamental opposition to this ancient paradigm when he awards a special place in God's realm to the poverty stricken, the hungry, and the tearful. In effect, he claims that the divine realm is peopled by the poor, the tearful, the hungry, and the persecuted. That claim stands the customary view on its head.

Kingdom and riches

Jesus' preference for the poor is confirmed by his harsh words for persons of wealth.

> It is easier for a camel to squeeze through a needle's eye, than for a wealthy person to get into God's domain.[12]

The Jesus tradition and modern scholars have struggled diligently to blunt the uncompromising tenor of this saying. One dodge

9. Deut 28:1–2
10. Deut 28:15

11. Deut 28:16–45
12. Mark 10:25//Matt 19:24// Luke18:25

was to argue that an Aramaic word meaning *rope* was mistranslated in Greek as *camel*; another was to suggest that there was a "camel gate" in the walls of Jerusalem that was narrow but large enough to allow a camel from to pass through if done so carefully. The hyperbole in this saying is characteristic of Jesus' tropes and so should be allowed to stand in its raw form.

Jesus reminds his followers that "It is very difficult for the rich to enter God's domain."[13] Jesus also caricatures the rich farmer (in Luke) and the big investor (in Thomas) who push greed and avarice to their limits only to die prematurely.[14] Finally, he issues a warning that service to God and preoccupation with wealth are incompatible:

> No one can be a slave to two masters. No doubt that slave will either hate one and love the other, or be devoted to one and disdain the other. You can't be enslaved to both God and a bank account.[15]

The word *mammon,* here translated as "bank account," is an Aramaic loanword in Greek, not original with Jesus. *Mammon* is a kind of pseudo-god, under whose spell one may readily fall. In so doing, one loses the ability to fasten exclusively on the true God. The Thomas version of the saying is preceded by this pronouncement: "A person cannot mount two horses, or bend two bows."[16] The single vision is not compatible with double loyalties, especially not when one of them is the pull of wealth.

The invisible realm of God is populated with the poor, the destitute, the tearful, the hungry, and, as we shall see, with unwanted children, in sum, with outsiders and outcasts. The entrance to that realm is sufficiently narrow to prevent those whose pockets bulge with money to squeeze through To be aware of that realm one has to have eyes wide open – eyes capable of catching a glimpse of what lies beyond the reigning view of the world. Such eyes are empowered by trust.

---

13. Matt 19:23   15. Matt 6:24
14. Luke 12:16–21//Thom 63:1–3   16. Thom 47:1

A
Trust
Ethic

Anxieties

Don't fret about your life – what you're going to eat and drink
– or about your body – what you're going to wear.

Source: Q • Matt 6:25

God & Birds

Take a look at the birds of the sky: they don't plant or harvest,
or gather into barns. Yet your heavenly Father feeds them.

Source Q • Matt 6:26

God & Lilies

Notice how the wild lilies grow: They don't slave and they never
spin.[29] Yet let me tell you, even Solomon at the height of his
glory was never decked out like one of them.

Source Q • Matt 6:28–29

God & Sparrows (1)

What do sparrows cost? A dime a dozen? Yet not one of them
is overlooked by God.

Source: Q • Luke 12:6

God & Sparrows (2)

What do sparrows cost? A penny apiece? Yet not one of them will
fall to the earth without the consent of your Father.

Source Q • Matt 10:29

God & Grass

If God dresses up the grass in the field, which is here today and
tomorrow is tossed into the oven, it is surely more likely that
God cares for you, you who don't take anything for granted!

Source Q • Luke 12:28

God & Hair

In fact, even the hairs of your head have been counted.

Source Q • Luke 12:7a

God & Crows

Think about the crows: they don't plant or harvest, they don't have store-rooms or barns. Yet God feeds them. You're worth a lot more than the birds!

Source: Q • Luke 12:24

Extending Life

Can any of you add an hour to life by fretting about it?

Source: Q • Luke 12:25

Bread for the Day

Provide us with the bread we need for the day.

Source: Q • Matt 6:11

Ask, Seek, Knock.

Ask – it'll be given to you; seek – you'll find; knock – it'll be opened for you. [10]Rest assured: everyone who asks receives; everyone who seeks finds; and for the one who knocks it will be opened.

Source: Q • Luke 11:9–10

Friend at Midnight

Jesus said to them, "Suppose you have a friend who comes to you in the middle of the night and says to you, 'Friend, lend me three loaves, [6]for a friend of mine on a trip has just shown up and I have nothing to offer him.' [7]And suppose you reply, 'Stop bothering me. The door is already locked and my children and I are in bed. I can't get up to give you anything' – [8]I tell you, even though you won't get up and give the friend anything out of friendship, yet you will get up and give the other whatever is needed because you'd be ashamed not to."

Source: Luke • Luke 11:5–8

A
Trust
Ethic

Trust is the horizon of God's domain and dominion. Trust forms the field of vision within which God's imperial rule is plainly visible. Trust is the door to the alternative reality that is God's domain.

The word we formerly used for trust was faith. But faith has been spoiled by its popular connotations. It has come to mean intellectual assent to the standard doctrines of one's religious tradition. When even more narrowly defined, faith means believing in believing. It is then regarded as a supernatural virtue that enables one to believe that God has revealed the divine will through Christ and the church. So we have come to speak of "faith traditions," which represent the compendia of convictions that characterizes particular religious communities.

Trust does not involve believing something or in something. Trust involves seeing the world and other people for what they are when viewed through God's eyes. Trust means acting on that perception. That is the heart of Jesus' vision.

Suppose you trust the view that the world is flat. Would you board a ship to sail around the world? Would you book a flight on an airplane that purports to take you to the other side of the globe? Or, to change the illustration, if you were not convinced that a medium could predict your future, would you pay her for advice? Trust means willingness to act on what you take to be ultimately true.

The contrast between endorsing traditional religious doctrines and trusting that the world is so constructed as to provide for the basic needs of birds and lilies becomes evident when we observe the consequences of that trust.

Most of us have been immersed in a work ethic: we labor to

produce the goods of life and the good life and believe our virtue resides largely in that labor. It is one of the legacies of the Enlightenment. In contrast, Jesus advocated and practiced a trust ethic.

He admonished his followers to take no thought for the morrow, for food, for clothing, for shelter. The flowers of the field and the birds of the sky were his paradigms of trust.[1] The need for food calls the birds to mind, the need for clothing reminds him of the lilies of the field. The birds and the flowers are devoid of anxiety about such things, and in God's domain so should humans be.

The providence of his Father, Jesus reasons, is evenly distributed over all life forms.

"What do sparrows cost?" he asks. "A dime a dozen? Yet not one of them is overlooked by God." "Indeed," he continues, "even the hairs on your head have been counted."

That attention to minute detail suggests how closely God monitors the creation. Then Jesus concludes, "You're worth more than a flock of sparrows."[2]

Anxieties about food and clothing constitute the acid test of a trust ethic. It is so basic to the vision of Jesus that he builds it into his prayer fragments. Like the Israelites wandering in the Sinai desert, disciples are never to ask for more than one day's bread at a time.

Luke 11:3

Provide us with the bread
we need day by day.

Matt 6:11

Provide us with the bread
we need for the day.

Did 8:2

Provide us with the bread
we need for the day.

---

1. Luke 12:22–25, 27–28   2. Luke 12:6–7

Matthew and Luke have taken their basic text from the Sayings Gospel Q. Luke has generalized, as he is wont to do, by having disciples ask for bread on a continuing basis. Matthew appears to have adhered to the Q text, which is probably from Jesus, and asked God only for bread for the day. No need, Jesus says, to look forward to tomorrow and the day after.

The Didache, an early second century catechetical work, has undoubtedly copied from Matthew. In contrast, Luke has taken the long view in revising the so-called Lord's Prayer. The Matthean form is more stringent: One is not to look beyond the present day. That calls for trust!

It is fairly easy to affirm trust in God. But if that trust means confidence in the behavior of fellow human beings, it is a much more demanding thing. For an itinerant, unfettered trust means this:

> ask – it'll be given you;
> seek – you'll find;
> knock – it'll be opened for you.[3]

As the tradition developed, this triple saying was given a vertical prayer context as the tradition developed (petitions addressed upward to God), but originally it was probably understood horizontally (requests addressed to people along the road) in connection with the wandering lifestyle of Jesus and his disciples. They had constant need for hospitality as they moved about the countryside.

As an itinerant, Jesus apparently trusted God absolutely. Trust in God translates in practice as trust in neighbor, in those one meets on the road, in the laws of hospitality. Such trust is suggested by the friend at midnight:

> Jesus said to them, "Suppose you have a friend who comes to you in the middle of the night and says to you, 'Friend, lend me three loaves, for a friend of mine on a trip has just shown up and I have nothing to offer him.' And suppose you reply, 'Stop bothering me. The door is already locked and my chil-

3. Luke 11:9–10

dren and I are in bed. I can't get up to give you anything' – I tell you, even though you won't get up and give the friend anything out of friendship, yet you will get up and give the other whatever is needed because you'd be ashamed not to."[4]

The door is already locked and the family has retired for the night. Then comes a knock on the door followed by a request for bread. Jesus invokes the laws of hospitality, which in this case obligate a neighbor to supply food for a weary traveler. The laws of hospitality are stronger than the claims of friendship. They override the inertia of inconvenience. The cameo in Appendix 1 illustrates the conviction that underlies the assurance, "knock – it'll be opened for you."

Among the instructions Jesus gave to his disciples as they departed on itinerant missions of their own, he suggests that they will be taken in and fed under the rules of hospitality. And in violation of the purity codes, he advises them to eat whatever is set before them. These practices, too, betray an attitude of utter trust.

Jesus considered preparations for the morrow and concern for food and clothing to betray a lack of trust. Although he knew very well that in the real world not everyone who asks receives. Yet he urged his followers to act with confidence that a request would bring a positive response. And he advocated reciprocity by admonishing his followers to give to every beggar who asks. That requires a huge affirmation of life in all its potentially beautiful aspects. But it entails the acceptance of life's ugly dimensions as well.

4. Luke 11:5–8

Celebration

3.

Dinner Party

Someone was giving a big dinner and invited many guests. [17]At the dinner hour the host sent his slave to tell the guests: "Come, it's ready now." [18]But one by one they all began to make excuses. The first said to him, "I just bought a farm, and I have to go and inspect it; please excuse me." [19]And another said, "I just bought five pairs of oxen, and I'm on my way to check them out; please excuse me." [20]And another said, "I just got married, and so I cannot attend." [21]So the slave came back and reported these <excuses> to his master. Then the master of the house got angry and instructed his slave: "Quick! Go out into the streets and alleys of the town, and usher in the poor, and crippled, the blind, and the lame."

[22]And the slave said, "Sir, your orders have been carried out, and there's still room."

[23]And the master said to the slave, "Then go out into the roads and the country lanes, and force people to come in so my house will be filled.

Sources: Q, Thomas • Luke 14:16–23

Lost Coin

Is there any woman with ten silver coins, who if she loses one, wouldn't light a lamp and sweep the house and search carefully until she finds it? [9]When she finds it, she invites her friends and neighbors over and says, 'Celebrate with me, because I have found the silver coin I had lost.'

Source: Luke • Luke 15:8–9

Lost Sheep

Is there any one of you who owns a hundred sheep and has one stray off, who wouldn't leave the ninety-nine in the wilderness, and go after the one that got lost until he finds it? [5]And when he finds it, he lifts it up on his shoulders, happy. [6]Once he gets home, he invites his friends and his neighbors over, and says to them, "Celebrate with me, because I have found my lost sheep."

Sources: Q, Thomas • Luke 15:4–6

Prodigal Son

Once there was this man who had two sons. [12]The younger of them said to his father, "Father, give me the share of the property that's coming to me." So he divided his resources between them.

[13]Not too many days later, the younger son got all his things together and left home for a faraway country, where he squandered his property by living extravagantly. [14]Just when he had spent it all, a serious famine swept through that country, and he began to do without. [15]So he went and hired himself out to one of the citizens of that country, who sent him out to his farm to feed the pigs. [16]He longed to satisfy his hunger with the carob pods, which the pigs usually ate; but no one offered him anything. [17]Coming to his senses he said, "Lots of my father's hired hands have more than enough to eat, while here I am dying of starvation! [18]I'll get up and go to my father and I'll say to him, 'Father, I have sinned against heaven and affronted you; [19]I don't deserve to be called a son of yours any longer; treat me like one of your hired hands.'" [20]And he got up and returned to his father.

But while he was still a long way off, his father caught sight of him and was moved to compassion. He went running out to him, threw his arms around his neck, and kissed him. [21]And the son said to him, "Father, I have sinned against heaven and affronted you; I don't deserve to be called a son of yours any longer."

[22]But the father said to his slaves, "Quick! Bring out the finest robe and put it on him; put a ring on his finger and sandals on his feet. [23]Fetch the fat calf and slaughter it; let's have a feast and celebrate, [24]because this son of mine was dead and has come back to life; he was lost and now is found." And they started celebrating.

[25]Now his elder son was out in the field; and as he got closer to the house, he heard music and dancing. [26]He called one of the servant boys over and asked what was going on.

[27]He said to him, "Your brother has come home and your father has slaughtered the fat calf, because he has him back safe and sound."

[28]But he was angry and refused to go in. So his father came out and began to plead with him. [29]But he answered his father, "See here, all these years I have slaved for you. I never once disobeyed any of your orders; yet you never once provided me with a kid goat so I could celebrate with my friends. [30]But when this son of yours shows

up, the one who has squandered your estate with prostitutes – for him you slaughter the fat calf."

³¹But <the father> said to him, "My child, you are always at my side. Everything that's mine is yours. ³²But we just had to celebrate and rejoice, because this brother of yours was dead, and has come back to life; he was lost, and now is found."

Source: Luke • Luke 15:11–32

Award to the Hungry

Congratulations, you hungry! You will have a feast.

Source: Q • Luke 6:21a

Award to the Tearful

Congratulations, you mourners! You will laugh.

Source: Q • Luke 6:21b

Fasting & Wedding

The groom's friends can't fast while the groom is present, can they?

Source: Mark • Mark 2:19

Able-bodied & Sick

And whenever the Pharisees' scholars saw him eating with sinners and toll collectors, they would question his disciples: "What's he doing eating with toll collectors and sinners?"

¹⁷When Jesus overhears, he says to them: "Since when do the able-bodied need a doctor? It's the sick who do."

Sources: Mark, GFragment 1224, common lore • Mark 2:16–17

Jesus and John the Baptist

We played the flute for you,
but you wouldn't dance;
we sang a dirge,
but you wouldn't weep.

³³Just remember, John the Baptist appeared on the scene, eating no bread and drinking no wine, and you say, 'He is demented.' ³⁴This mother's son appeared on the scene both eating and drinking, and you say, 'There's a glutton and a drunk, a crony of toll collectors and sinners.

Source: Q • Luke 7:32–34

Celebration

Since God's domain is hidden, it is a fiction to be embraced on trust. To trust means to act as though something were true even when the evidence is ambiguous or marginal. Human beings can embrace a fiction only if it is undergirded by faith, to use the older term in a precise sense. Celebration is the by-product of that trust. In other words, celebration is the endorsement of trust. Celebration nourishes trust. Celebration is the heart of liturgy in God's domain.

One reason many of us in the Seminar believe Jesus could not have been an apocalyptic prophet who expected the world to end momentarily is his impulse to celebrate. Apocalyptic is for those who mourn the corruption of creation, who think they have been cheated in the game of life; it is not a program for the future; it is the counsel of endtime despair. In the so-called little apocalypse in Mark 13, we are told "For those days will see distress the likes of which has not occurred since God created the world until now, and will never occur again."[1] The calamities of the endtime will be pervasive: "For nation will rise up against nation and empire against empire; there will be earthquakes everywhere; there will be famines."[2] The suffering will be so great that "One brother will turn in another to be put to death, and a father his child, and children will turn against their parents and kill them."[3] Trust will be a minor commodity under apocalyptic distress. The contrast between the apocalyptic mentality and the disposition of the authentic Jesus is nowhere more striking than on this point.

Celebration runs like a Dionysian thread through the authentic stories and witticisms of Jesus. The theme is especially promi-

1. Mark 13:19
2. Mark 13:8
3. Mark 13:12

nent in his narrative parables: the dinner party, the lost coin, the lost sheep, and the lost son (the prodigal).

The dinner party survived in the Jesus tradition in three forms. Matthew, Luke, and Thomas have construed it in accordance with their special interests. Behind the three versions, however, a single plot is discernible. We cannot be certain of the details, of course, but the trend of the story seems clear enough. In the story as Jesus probably told it, a host of some means gives a dinner party and invites an unspecified number of guests. At the hour of the banquet, the host sends a servant around to collect the guests, in accordance with ancient custom. But they offer what appear to be contrived excuses for not coming. The host then orders the servant to go out into the high roads and the lanes and collect all sorts of people. These chance invitees become privileged guests, hinting at a symposium, an evening of conviviality. Dinner for a handful is transformed into a banquet for dozens.[4]

The theme is of course celebration. But the celebration embraces people on an indiscriminate basis. No doubt there were poor among the second class guests, but there may also have been persons of means and even the wealthy. Thomas excludes merchants and the artisan class in his version. Luke prefers the poor, the crippled, the blind, and the lame in his version of God's domain. They constitute his favorite groups. Matthew has turned the story into a royal banquet and the parable turns out to be an allegory of the history of salvation. Luke may, in fact, have kept closest to the original version.

It is clear that Jesus often looked at the world through the eyes of persons with means. That is evident in the dinner party, in the prodigal, in the shrewd manager,[5] in the vineyard laborers,[6] in the pearl,[7] in the treasure,[8] and in the rich farmer,[9] as well as the unforgiving slave.[10] Accordingly, it is not unreasonable to assume that he dined upon occasion with the wealthy and the powerful.

4. Luke 14:16–24//Thom 64:1–12// Matt 22:1–14
5. Luke 16:1–8a
6. Matt 20:1–15
7. Thom 76:1–2
8. Matt 13:44
9. Thom 63:1–4
10. Matt 18:23–34

He seems willing enough to take a handout wherever he can get it.

The dinner party is thus a parable of radical inclusiveness. It excludes only those who do not recognize the potential of the occasion, who are preoccupied with the cares of the world. The open table is both the reason for and the means of celebration.

There is also comedy in Jesus' stories of celebration. The celebration may be incommensurate with the treasure recovered. A woman loses one of ten coins, and sweeps the dirt floor of her house to find it. She then spends her newfound coin to celebrate her good fortune.

A shepherd goes in search of a wayward sheep, which has wandered off from a flock of one hundred. He seems indifferent to the flock as he searches for the stray. When he finds it he calls for a celebration, which in his culture normally required the slaughter of a lamb.

The younger son squanders his share of his patrimony on prostitutes in a foreign land and is forced to feed the pigs in his new poverty. Shamed and penniless, the prodigal returns home destitute and penitent. The father welcomes him as though he were a visiting potentate and throws an elaborate party for him. The older son, who has labored steadily in the meantime, demurs at what for him was unwarranted extravagance.[11]

In all these stories, Jesus is a celebrant of life, life replete with ups and downs, ins and outs, successes and disappointments. He was a celebrant of the fiction of God's reign. *L'chaim! (To Life!)*

Celebration consists of feasting and laughter. God's reign is inimical to hunger and sadness. To the hungry, Jesus gives this assurance:

Congratulations, you hungry! You will have a feast.[12]

To those in mourning, this is his promise:

Congratulations, you who weep now! You will laugh.[13]

---

11. Luke 15:11–32   12. Luke 6:21a   13. Luke 6:21b

We will subsequently return to the observation that Jesus was something of a comic. Laughter played a large role in his brand of wisdom. But so did poverty and hunger and sadness and suffering. Those so afflicted are the special beneficiaries of God's rule. They are to celebrate their inclusion with feasting and laughter.

Jesus apparently dined frequently with toll collectors and sinners. According to Mark,

> And whenever the Pharisees' scholars saw him eating with sinners and toll collectors, they would question his disciples, "What's he doing eating with toll collectors and sinners?"
>
> When Jesus overhears, he says to them: "Since when do the able-bodied need a doctor? It's the sick who do."[14]

Those who are well have no reason to seek the services of a physician. But the sick do. On the assumption that toll collectors and sinners were the religiously and morally "ill" in his society, he assigns himself to their case — metaphorically speaking. It is of course a jest, but a jest is just what the doctor ordered.

The affliction of much contemporary religiosity, especially of the moralistic variety, is that it is humorless. If we cannot laugh at ourselves and even about the things we hold dear, then God's reign has eluded us.

The behavior of Jesus is contrasted with that of John the Baptist. The disciples of John the Baptist fast and so do the Pharisees, but Jesus and his disciples do not fast. To this observation Jesus responds, "The groom's friends can't fast while the groom is around, can they? So long as the groom is around, you can't expect them to fast."[15] A wedding and fasting are simply incompatible. The Jesus movement renewed the practice of fasting not long after Jesus' death. In accordance with that renewal, custodians of the tradition added a correction: "[20]But the days will come when the groom is taken away from them, and then they will fast on that day." Jesus has now become the groom, and

14. Mark 2:16–17a   15. Mark 2:19

since he is gone, it is proper to resume fasting. The tradition modifies itself to reflect current practice in the emerging church.

The styles of Jesus and John are contrasted in a passage Luke and Matthew have taken from Q:

> John the Baptist appeared on the scene, eating no bread and drinking no wine, and you say, "He is demented." This mother's son appeared on the scene both eating and drinking, and you say, "There is a glutton and a drunk, a crony of toll collectors and sinners."[16]

The Baptist is said to have a demon because he was a strict ascetic. In the Baptist movement, as quickly as you can say 'John the Baptist,' you're up to your groin in sackcloth and ashes! In the Jesus movement, by way of contrast, you're immediately into feasting and drinking. As a consequence of the contrast, Jesus gained the reputation of a glutton and a drunk. During an interview, I quoted the passage cited above to a reporter in Australia. The next morning the headline to the story about the Jesus Seminar read: "Scholar says Jesus was a drunk." The orthodox fasters must have winced at the thought that Jesus might have been a partygoer and the least bit frivolous. So the reporter attributed the remark to me rather than to the ancient gospels.

16. Luke 7:31–35//Matt 11:16–19

Outsiders & Outcasts

Prophets without Honor; Doctors without Cures

Jesus said, "No prophet is welcome on his home turf; ²doctors don't cure those who know them."

Sources: Thomas, Mark, John • Thom 31:1–2

Foxes & Birds

Foxes have dens, and the birds of the sky have nests; but this mother's son has nowhere to rest his head.

Sources: Q, Thomas • Luke 9:58

Inside & Outside

Jesus said, "Why do you wash the outside of the cup?² Don't you understand that the one who made the inside is also the one who made the outside?"

Sources: Thomas, Q • Thom 89:1–2

For & Against

In fact, whoever is not against us is on our side.

Sources: Mark, Q • Mark 9:40

Children

Let the children come up to me, don't try to stop them. After all, God's domain is peopled with such as these.

Source: Mark • Mark 10:14b

Lepers

Then a leper comes up to him, pleads with him, falls down on his knees, and says to him, "If you want to, you can make me clean."

⁴¹Although Jesus was indignant, he stretched out his hand, touched him, and says to him, "Okay – you're clean!"

⁴²And right away the leprosy disappeared, and he was

made clean. [43]And Jesus snapped at him, and dismissed him curtly [44]with this warning: "See that you don't tell anyone anything, but go, have a priest examine <your skin>. Then offer for your cleansing what Moses commanded, as evidence <of your cure>."

[45]But after he went out, he started telling everyone and spreading the story, so that <Jesus> could no longer enter a town openly, but had to stay out in the countryside. Yet they continued to come to him from everywhere.

Sources: Mark, Egerton Gospel • Mark 1:40–45

Toll Collectors & Prostitutes

Jesus said to them, "I swear to you, the toll collectors and prostitutes will get into God's domain, but you will not."

Source: Matthew • Matt 21:31b

Outsiders & Outcasts

Jesus as outsider

Jesus apparently regarded himself as an outsider. He was in exile from his hometown, from his friends and neighbors. This two-line saying preserved by the Gospel of Thomas sums up the situation:

> No prophet is welcome on his home turf;
> doctors don't cure those who know them.[1]

Some form of this saying is recorded in all five gospels. The connection between prophets and doctors is preserved in Luke:

> And he said to them, "No doubt you will quote me this proverb, 'Doctor, cure yourself,' and you'll tell me, 'Do here in your hometown what we've heard you've done in Capernaum.'" Then he said, "The truth is, no prophet is welcome on his home turf."[2]

In Capernaum he had cured the sick. He was expected to repeat the performance in Nazareth but did not. Mark has expanded the audience that fails to honor its own prophetic voices:

> Jesus used to tell them: "No prophet goes without respect, except on his home turf and among his relatives and at home!"[3]

Among those who withhold honor from prophets, Mark has included Jesus' relatives – mother and siblings – who apparently did not honor him at first because they thought he was mad. [4]The greatest wound of all is to be snubbed by parents and siblings.

The tradition moved his birthplace from Nazareth to Bethlehem, partly because the messiah was to be born in Bethlehem

1. Thom 31:1–2
2. Luke 4:23–24
3. Mark 6:4
4. Mark 3:21

according to the prophecy, and partly because Nazareth had disowned him.

Jesus was an itinerant, which means that he was a guest, a traveler, a stranger, an alien in most contexts. He did not have a home, although he may have worked out of certain centers, such as Capernaum. His life as a wanderer is confirmed by another saying found in both the Sayings Gospel Q and the Gospel of Thomas:

> Foxes have dens, and the birds of the sky have nests;
> but this mother's son has nowhere to rest his head.[5]

Homeless, he depended on the graciousness of those he met along the way to supply him with food and drink and a place to sleep. A number of his sayings cluster around this aspect of his existence, especially those that express his ethic of trust.

Outcasts

In a well-ordered society, people know their places. In Jesus' world the few very rich and the many very poor knew their places. The social distance between them was mediated by brokers who dispensed favors bestowed by patrons on compliant artisans and peasants and peons. Social stratification was enforced by the purity codes, which segregated lepers, women, children, petty tax officials, demoniacs, the physically handicapped, and gentiles.

An aphorism preserved in Thom 89 suggests that Jesus is the universal barrier breaker:

> Why do you wash the outside of the cup?
> Don't you understand that the one who made the inside is also the one who made the outside?[6]

The initial rhetorical question is nonsensical. People do not wash merely the outside of cups. It is as though Jesus is imputing

5. Luke 9:57
6. Thom 89:1–2

to them a practice that is absurd. One cannot wash the outside without also washing the inside. The second question shifts the focus from the outside/inside contrast to the potter who made both the inside and the outside. The saying is thus an attack on the distinction itself. A community without insiders and outsiders is a community under the aegis of the maker who made them both.

This saying is taken up in the Q tradition where it is moralized and applied to the Pharisees.[7] The opponents of the new movement are now characterized as those who wash the outside of cups but leave the inside full of greed and evil. This development reflects the tension in the later community and turns the original sense of the saying on its head.

An anecdote reported by Mark depicts the disciples as attempting to draw a line between an outsider performing exorcisms in Jesus' name and insiders doing the same thing. To their complaint Jesus responds:

> Don't stop him! After all, no one who performs a miracle in my name will turn around the next moment and curse me. In fact, whoever is not against us is on our side.[8]

This response is copied by Luke[9] but omitted by Matthew. In a different context, the saying is attributed to Jesus in the gospel fragment known as Papyrus Oxyrhynchus 1224:

> And pray for your enemies. For the one who is not against you is on your side. The one who today is at a distance, tomorrow will be near you.[10]

The expulsion of demons was a manifestation of the arrival of God's imperial rule, no matter whose hand was symbolically responsible. POxy 1224 even links this inclusiveness to enemies. Nevertheless, once the community began to define its limits, the barriers went up. The for/against aphorism is in fact turned around:

---

7. Luke 11:39–41//Matt 23:25–26   9. Luke 9:50
8. Mark 9:40   10. POxy 1224 6:1–2

The one who isn't with me is against me,
and the one who doesn't gather with me scatters.[11]

This saying is taken from Q.

In a number of his sayings he embraces the beggars, the poor, the hungry, the mournful as he moves about Galilee. He becomes known as a friend of toll collectors and sinners – those who fall outside the boundaries of acceptable company. Jesus appears to ignore the social boundaries of his society in the most radical manner. In this chapter, we take note especially of his attitude toward women, children, lepers, and toll collectors.

Women

As a friend of those on the margins of society, it is easy to believe that he had women in his public retinue. We cannot be certain, but it seems likely that some women followed him about. That may be the reason some of his followers were classified as "toll collectors and whores." The slogan—it is no more than that— was applied to persons regarded as the riff-raff of society, those of lower social status. The application of the cliché to women may mean no more than that these women violated the social code by following Jesus around in public.

Not all women in Jesus' society were marginalized. Some women in the Roman world were wealthy and influential. Some of the women in Jesus' retinue may have been of sufficient means to support his itinerant lifestyle. Sages often embrace poverty as protection against self-aggrandizement. Mahatma Gandhi is a modern sage who adopted this protective shield. When Gandhi died, his estate is reported to have been worth three dollars. Yet Gandhi had many friends who supported him. One of Gandhi's followers once remarked: "Gandhi has no idea how much it costs to keep him in poverty." Jesus probably falls into this category. His trust ethic may have been silently undergirded by the women around him.

11. Luke 11:23//Matt 12:30

Children

Birth in the Roman world was more than a biological occurrence. The birth of a child had to be affirmed by the head of the family and thus was also a social act. Following birth, the father "raised the child" up if he wanted to acknowledge it as his own; he did so by retrieving the child from the ground where the midwife had placed it and cradling it in his arms. The gesture also indicated his unwillingness to have it exposed.

The scene depicted in the Gospel of Mark is reminiscent of that gesture.

> And they would bring children to him so he could lay hands on them, but the disciples scolded them. Then Jesus grew indignant when he saw this and said to them: "Let the children come up to me, don't try to stop them. After all, God's domain is peopled with such as these. I swear to you, whoever doesn't accept God's imperial rule the way a child would, certainly won't ever set foot in his domain!" And he would put his arms around them and bless them, and lay his hands on them.[12]

The declaration of Jesus identifies children as one of the basic components of the population of God's domain. By embracing the children and touching them, he indicates they are to be recognized and claimed as bona fide participants in the family of God.

This symbolic act is to be viewed in sharp contrast to the status of some children in the Roman world. Malformed infants were regularly exposed or drowned. Girl babies more often went unclaimed by their fathers than boys. A father away from home for an extended period might order his pregnant wife to abandon her baby. Similarly, the babies of wayward daughters were left to the elements. Poor families commonly abandoned children they could not afford to raise, and even wealthy families might expose a child who posed a problem for the probate of an estate.

12. Mark 10:13–16

Abortion, exposure, and infanticide were common practice and entirely legal.

According to Mark (in the passage quoted above), the disciples of Jesus apparently had difficulty accepting exposed infants into the new community of faith. The memory of Jesus' example prompted some to welcome such children. But there is also a hint that the reception of children was the paradigm for the formal entrance of children into the church via baptism, an analogy that is developed in the Gospel of John.[13] While the framework of this anecdote about Jesus receiving and blessing the children is undoubtedly Markan, the core saying may well reflect a memory of the historical Jesus.

Lepers

By definition, lepers were outcasts in Jesus' society. They were quarantined, so to speak, because they were considered unclean. Contact with an unclean person disqualified one for normal social relationships and religious observances. We do not know what actually happened to the leper Jesus is reported to have cured in the Gospel of Mark.[14] But Jesus pronounces the leper clean and thereby restores him to full standing in human society. He thereby usurps the priestly function and declares the leper clean on the spot. He acts before and after on his own pronouncements: he had already socialized with lepers; he restores this leper to society; he continues to socialize with lepers.

Toll Collectors

Toll collectors were normally Jews who had become tax-farmers for the Romans – or in Galilee for Herod Antipas. The job of toll collectors was to collect tolls and tariffs on commerce and goods passing through toll stations such as Capernaum and Jericho. They gained the unsavory reputation they had because they were unethical, given to abuse and dishonesty. Their bad

13. John 3:3–5   14. Mark 1:40–45

reputation is reflected in John the Baptist's advice to them: "Charge nothing above the official rates."[15] A chief toll collector like Zacchaeus would have agents working under him.[16] Zacchaeus was apparently an exception to the rule that toll collectors were dishonest: He offers publicly to pay back four times any amount he is supposed to have extorted.

Toll collectors are linked with sinners,[17] with whores,[18] and with gentiles or pagans.[19] They thus belong to the excluded class of Jews who did not follow the Pharisaic interpretation of the purity codes.

Toll collectors appear in three different levels of the tradition. If we are correct in assuming with Mark[20] and the Sayings Gospel Q[21] that Jesus associated openly at table with toll collectors and sinners, he must have regarded them positively as belonging to that category of persons to whom God's domain belonged by virtue of their social status. This would reflect the earliest stage of the Jesus tradition.

Jesus' contemporaries would have had a negative opinion of toll collectors and those associated with them. That view of them is reflected in John the Baptist's admonition to them cited above.[22] It is carried over into the later Christian community in this piece of advice regarding the unruly: "Then if he or she refuses to listen to them [one or two other members of the group], report it to the congregation. If he or she refuses to listen even to the congregation, treat that companion like you would a pagan or toll collector."[23] This negative view may also lie at the base of a saying recorded by Matthew: "If you love those who love you, why should you be commended for that? Even the toll collectors do as much don't they?"[24] They are compared in parallel rhetorical questions with the gentiles or pagans: "And if you

15. Luke 3:12
16. Luke 19:1–10
17. Mark 2:15//Matt 9:11//Luke 5:30
18. Matt 21:31b
19. Matt 18:17
20. Mark 2:15–17//
  Matt 9:10–13//Luke 5:29–32
21. Q Luke 7:31–34//
  Matt 11:18–19
22. Luke 3:12
23. Matt 18:15–17
24. Matt 5:46

The Fate of Girl Babies

Stories from two ancient authors, Ovid and Apuleius, illustrate how girl babies were regarded and how in some rare instances they escaped the fate intended for them. In one a miracle is involved, in a second the girl eventually meets the fate intended originally for her.

The Fate of Iphis

Ovid (43 B.C.E.–17 C.E.) was a Latin poet and contemporary of Jesus. He was banished by Augustus to a town near the Black Sea. His most famous work is *Metamorphoses*, written 1–8 C.E.

Ligdus was married to Telethusa, who was pregnant. He prayed for two things: that she would be delivered of her child with the least pain, and that she would give birth to a boy. The reason, he opined, is that girls are more expensive to raise and provide a dowry for. So he gives the order, "If is girl is born, she is to be put to death." Ligdus told his wife he did not want to do this, so he prayed to be forgiven. But his mind was made up. And he departed on a journey.

The goddess Io, another name for Osiris, appears to Telethusa in a dream. She instructs Telethusa not to follow her husband's orders, but to rear the girl as a boy. She names the child Iphis, which is a name suitable for either a boy or a girl.

When the girl reaches the age of thirteen, the father arranges a marriage for her with Ianthus, who is of course a girl. They two fall in love. Was it to be a lesbian relationship? By no means. Iphis imagines her love to be that of a boy for this charming girl, and Ianthus imagines her love to be for a husband. On the occasion of the wedding, which Iphis' mother has postponed innumerable times for fear of discovery, Iphis is filled with anticipated passion. And the goddess once more comes to the rescue. Isis transforms Iphis into a male just in time for the wedding night.

Ovid, *Metamorphoses*, Book IX.675–79.

The Brother, the Sister, and the Jealous Wife

Lucius Apuleius (ca. 124–170) was a north African philosopher and teacher of rhetoric. He wrote commentaries and a bawdy novel, *The Golden Ass*. The tale of the ill-fated girl baby is found in that work.

The story in Apuleius is tragic. Here is a narrative summary.

The father is away, as is often the case, on a journey leaving a pregnant wife behind. He has given orders that the child is to be put to death if it is a girl. But mother love is too strong, and the mother, after giving birth, entrusts the girl to a neighbor to raise. Upon his return the husband is told that it was indeed a girl and that she has been exposed.

The girl grows up, as girls will do. She becomes of marriageable age. Because she lacks a dowry (her foster parents are poor), she is unable to marry. The mother then reveals the secret to her son, the brother of the daughter allegedly put to death. The brother, who is married, takes his sister into his family as a girl from the neighborhood who has no parents. He treats her with great respect. As it is time for her to marry, the brother marries her to a close friend and gives her a generous dowry.

It would seem that the story will have a happy ending. But that is not to be the case. The brother's wife

Continued next page

Fate of Girl Babies, continued

discerns a certain affection of her husband for his sister, whom she takes to be a secret lover and no relative at all. To prove their relationship, she devises a tryst, the token of which was to be her husband's ring, which the sister would of course recognize when presented by the messenger. When the unwary girl arrives at the scene of the tryst, the jealous wife confronts her, and has her stripped and beaten. She eventually puts her to death with a hot poker.

The story does not end here. The woman devises a whole series of murders to insure that she will inherit her husband's wealth. But she is eventually detected and on the order of the governor is thrown to the wild beasts, a suitable ending, it seems, for so vicious a life.

Apuleius, *The Golden Ass, 23–28.*

greet only your friends, what have you done that is exceptional? Even the pagans do as much don't they?"[25] In the parallel passages, Luke substitutes "sinners" both times.[26] Matthew's version is undoubtedly derived from Q and may ultimately go back to Jesus. If we are to understand the comparison as one constructed by Jesus, we have to take it as a bit of irony: (with a wink at his audience,) "Given your view of toll collectors, isn't it surprising that they behave so well?" If this saying is not ironic, we must assume that it reflects the negative view of toll collectors adopted during the second stage of the tradition.

At a third level of understanding, toll collectors have become the model for humble and repentant Christians. There is no longer any social reality in the designation. It has become a metaphor for the proper attitude. The primary example is perhaps the equation of Matthew the toll collector with Levi in the call of one of the first disciples.[27] Only the Gospel of Matthew

25. Matt 5:4   27. Mark 2:14//Matt 9:9//Luke
26. Luke 6:32–33   5:29

identifies Levi with Matthew, although it is assumed that Levi is a toll collector since he is giving a dinner for toll collectors and others. The author of Matthew apparently has a special interest in identifying one of the twelve as a toll collector. If that identification is correct, that would be another reason for thinking Jesus may have had a positive attitude toward toll collectors.

The third level of understanding is also mirrored in the parable of the Pharisee and the toll collector[28] and the account of Zacchaeus, the chief toll collector, referred to earlier.[29] Zacchaeus is exonerated because he gives liberally to the poor and because he offers to pay a fourfold restitution for any amount he has extorted from anyone. Luke further identifies toll collectors with repentant sinners in the introduction to a series of parables.[30] By the time Luke gets through with the phrase, the last ounce of reality has been drained out of it. Such are the vicissitudes of the tradition.

Sayings in which toll collectors appear reflect three different levels of the Jesus tradition as it unfolds:

1. Jesus has a positive regard for toll collectors.
2. Jesus' contemporaries had a negative view of toll collectors.
3. The phrase toll collector becomes a metaphor for the humble and repentant Christian.

These differences provide valuable clues to the various stages of the tradition.

The invisible domain of God is populated with the poor, the destitute, with women and unwanted children, with lepers, and toll collectors, all considered under some circumstances to be the dregs of society. They are outsiders and outcasts. They are exiles from their native religious tradition. No wonder Jesus' auditors were puzzled by his vision of the population of God's domain — it contradicted their normal notion of who belonged and who did not, of who was in and who was out.

---

28. Luke 18:10–13
29. Luke 19:1–10

30. Luke 15:1, 7, 10: lost sheep, lost coin, prodigal

Transcending Tribalism

5.

Love of Enemies

Love your enemies. Pray for those who abuse you.

Source: Q • Luke 6:27–28

Merit in Love

If you love those who love you, why should you be commended for that? Even the toll collectors do as much, don't they?

Source: Q • Matt 5:46

Children of the Father

You'll then become children of your Father.

Source: Q • Matt 5:45a

Sun & Rain

God causes the sun to rise on both the bad and the good, and sends rain on both the just and the unjust.

Source: Q • Matt 5:45b

The Samaritan

This fellow was on his way from Jerusalem down to Jericho when he fell into the hands of robbers. They stripped him, beat him up, and went off, leaving him half dead. [31]Now by coincidence a priest was going down that road; when he caught sight of him, he went out of his way to avoid him. [32]In the same way, when a Levite came to the place, he took one look at him and crossed the road to avoid him. [33]But this Samaritan who was traveling that way came to where he was and was moved to pity at the sight of him. [34]He went up to him and bandaged his wounds, pouring olive oil and wine on them. He hoisted him onto his own animal, brought him to an inn, and looked after him. [35]The next day he took out two silver coins, which he gave to the innkeeper, and said, "Look after him, and on my way back I'll reimburse you for any extra expense you have had."

Source: Luke • Luke 10:30–35

On Divorce

"Everyone who divorces his wife and marries another commits adultery; and the one who marries a woman divorced from her husband commits adultery."

Luke 16:18

"But I tell you: Everyone who divorces his wife (except in the case of infidelity) makes her the victim of adultery; and whoever marries a divorced woman commits adultery."

Matt 5:32

And he says to them, "Whoever divorces his wife and marries another commits adultery against her; [12]and if she divorces her husband and marries another, she commits adultery."

Mark 10:11–12

"Now I say to you, whoever divorces his wife, except for infidelity, and marries another commits adultery."

Matt 19:9

Castration for Heaven

There are castrated men who were born that way, and there are castrated men who were castrated by others, and there are castrated men who castrated themselves because of Heaven's imperial rule.

Source: Matthew • Matt 19:12

Transcending Tribalism

Love your enemies

Somewhere near the heart of Jesus' vision is this simple admonition that from the very first has inspired and troubled his followers: love your enemies.

  This is an action statement: it recommends that the followers of Jesus perform some deed, presumably some activity appropriate to God's domain. If we take the rhetorical complex in which this saying is embedded as a faithful exposition of the sense of the admonition, then we would have to say that loving one's enemies imitates the divine disposition. A little later in the Q sequence, we are told:

> If you love those who love you, why should you be commended for that?
> Even toll collectors do as much, don't they?[1]
> If you love your enemies, *"you'll become children of your Father."*[2]
> As you know The Most High is equally generous to the ungrateful and the wicked?[3]

Or as Matthew has it:

> God causes the sun to rise on both the bad and the good,
> and sends rain on both the just and the unjust. [4]

That's the basis of a fairly radical notion of God. A God who treats all human beings evenhandedly is not in much evidence in either testament. The God pictured in the Bible is highly partial and often quite vindictive. The God of Jesus, in contrast, appears to have no favorites. The cosmic background of life is apparently neutral and therefore inclusive.

1. Matt 5:46   3. Luke 6:35b
2. Matt 5:45   4. Matt 5:45b

The jealous God of Israel, the God of the covenant, is inclined to favoritism on behalf of Israel and an enemy of the pagan peoples. It comes to graphic expression in Psalm 110:

> The Lord said to my lord,
> Sit here at my right,
> until I turn your enemies into a footrest.
> . . . .
> The Lord at your right hand will crush kings on the day of his wrath;
> He will pronounce judgment on the nations;
> he will fill them with corpses;
> he will smash the heads of many on the earth.[5]

When Matthew quotes this Psalm, his version is slightly different:

> The Lord said to my lord,
> sit here at my right,
> until I make your enemies grovel at your feet.[6]

In this passage and hundreds of others in the Old Testament, the enemies are the foes of Israel, the pagan city-states and nations. Enmity between and among tribes and ethnic groups was the rule rather than the exception. This understanding is reiterated in the birth and childhood stories preserved by Luke:

> This is what is promised in the words of his holy prophets of old: [71]deliverance from our enemies, and from the hands of all who hate us; [72]mercy to our ancestors, and the remembrance of his holy covenant. [73]This is the oath he swore to Abraham our ancestor: [74]to grant that we be rescued from the hands of our enemies, to serve him without fear.[7]

As we shall note below, the motivation for the creation of abundant progeny of the male gender was the protection of the tribe against its foes. Thus, the exhortation to multiply and fill the earth was a tribal charge, not a mandate for all of humankind.

---

5. Psalm 110:1, 4–6; LXX 109:1, 5–6   7. Luke 1:70–74
6. Matt 22:44

In a world emerging from tribal cultures, Jesus' admonition to love enemies must have struck his hearers as truly radical. In formulating it, Jesus is marking the transition from the ethnic phase of human societies to the transethnic phase, as Lloyd Geering puts it.[8] No longer was it ethnic identity to be the primary focus; instead, what human beings had in common, rather than what defined their differences, became the central concern. Jesus was apparently among those who saw the great change coming. Of course, we have not made a great deal of progress in the last two millennia, but even so we are now on the verge of the next phase of our development, the beginning of the global phase. It seems we never catch up.

When Matthew and Luke took the saying, "Love your enemies," from Q, they understood it to refer to personal enemies rather than enemies of the group. In the complex Luke has assembled, for example, the personal enemy is the focus:

Love your enemies,
do favors for those who hate you,
bless those who curse you,
pray for those who abuse you.
When someone strikes you on the cheek,
offer the other as well.
If someone takes away your coat,
don't prevent that person from taking your shirt along with it.
Give to everyone who begs from you;
and when someone takes your things,
don't ask for them back.
Treat people the way you want them to treat you.[9]

The climax in the golden rule makes it abundantly clear that the passage is concerned with individual enemies rather than enemies of the tribe or state. Yet on the lips of Jesus in Galilee in the first century, the focus may well have been on the oppressors of the group. For example, it is likely that the Romans and the upper classes among the Galileans were the oppressors, and the poverty stricken peasants were the friends of Jesus were the

8. *The World to Come*, p. 100–121.   9. Luke 6:27–31

oppressed. The series of examples in Luke and Matthew suggest the foreign oppressor: a humiliating strike on the cheek by a superior, an aggressive suit for an outer garment in satisfaction of a debt,[10] and Matthew's "If anyone conscripts you for one mile, go along for two"[11] betrays the presence of a foreigner oppressor, probably the Romans. Luke may have omitted the admonition about an extra mile from his list to avoid offending his Roman readers.

But whether the enemy was personal or collective, love your enemies is probably the most radical thing Jesus ever said. It is clear that he was quite ready to relocate social boundary markers, often in a very radical, impractical way. And it seems equally clear that the generosity extended to tribal foes was to be offered to personal foes as well.

That tribal enemies rather than personal enemies were the focus of Jesus' concern is demonstrated by the parable of the good Samaritan. In that parable, the enemy is the Samaritan, whose tribe had been at metaphorical and actual war with the Judeans for many centuries. (For more on this point, see the cameo essay on the Samaritan in Appendix 2.)

Divorce, polygamy, procreation & the future of the tribe

Jesus lived in a time when tribal and ethnic boundaries were being threatened on every hand. On the one side, they were threatened from without by paganism and Graeco-Roman culture generally, which were permeating older tribal and ethnic traditions. On the other, tribal solidarity was being compromised from within by the parties and sects in Judaism that vied with each other for ascendancy. Jesus himself contributed to the dissolution of tribal culture by his attitude toward the alien enemy, and by his strictures on the power of the patriarch within family structures (Chapter 6, *Kinship in God's Domain*).

10. Luke 6:29   11. Matt 5:41

In the ethnic age, the future of the tribe depended upon prolific reproduction: child-bearing was essential to the life and success of the tribe in relation to other tribes. The creation story in Genesis was invoked as justification for the tribal perspective. Had God not commanded Adam and Eve, "Be fruitful and multiply, and fill the earth and subdue it"? The family structure was similar in the settling of the American West: a large family was essential to survival and success. The immigrant literature depicting the struggles of families to carve out a living on the high plains in North America testifies to the need for children as co-laborers in the arduous tasks with which pioneers were faced, especially in the first years.

In ancient Israel, both divorce and polygamy were regarded as essential to insure the future of the tribe. If a wife could not bear children, the husband had the right, nay, the duty to take a second wife to bear him children, or to divorce his barren wife and replace her with one who was fertile. According to Elaine Pagels, "Jewish custom banned as 'abominations' sexual acts not conducive to procreation, and the impurity laws even prohibited marital intercourse except at times most likely to result in conception."[12] The rabbis taught that the production of progeny took precedence over obligations to a barren wife.

Jesus appears to have challenged those ancient mores designed to protect the propagation of the tribe. When asked whether divorce was permitted, he responded:

"What did Moses command you?"

They replied, "Moses allowed one to prepare a written decree and thus to divorce the other party."

Jesus said to them, "He gave you this injunction because you are obstinate. However, in the beginning, at the creation, 'God made them male and female. For that reason, a man will leave his father and mother and be united with his wife, and the two will become one body.' so they are no longer two individuals but 'one body.' Therefore those God has coupled together, no one else should separate."[13]

12. *Adam, Eve & the Serpent*, p. 11.   13. Mark 10:3–9

Early Christian Moral Instruction

The Shepherd of Hermas is a second-century work designed to serve as instruction for catechumens. The book is divided into three parts: Visions, Mandates, Similitudes. The section on chastity is taken from the Mandates.

"I order you," he says, "to practice chastity and not permit the thought to enter your mind to commit adultery with another man's wife, or to engage in sex <with another woman>, or to contemplate other such comparable wicked acts. If you do so, you will be committing a grievous sin. However, if you keep your own wife in mind you will avoid sin. ²For if your mind is filled with lust, you will certainly sin, and if you perform other wicked acts, you commit sin. Lust is a serious sin for the servant of God. If anyone commits this wicked deed, he or she brings about death for him or herself. ³Therefore, be on guard: abstain from lust, for where holiness resides, there is no room for immorality." ⁴I say to him, "Lord, permit me to ask you a few questions." "Go ahead," he replies. "Lord," I continue, "if a man has a wife of faith in the Lord and he discovers that she has committed some act of adultery, is the husband committing sin by continuing to live with her?" ⁵"So long as he is ignorant of her adultery, he does not sin," he responds. "But if the husband discovers her unfaithfulness, and she does not repent, but continues

One could translate: "They are one body, one person." Accordingly, in Mark, Jesus prohibits divorce altogether. When Matthew revises Mark, he adds an exception, "except in the case of infidelity," an exception the Fellows of the Jesus Seminar

her adulterous relationship, and the husband continues to live with her, then he shares in her adultery." ⁶"What then should the husband do," I ask, "if his wife persists in indulging her passion?" "Divorce her," he responds, "and live alone. If the husband divorces his wife and marries another, he commits adultery himself." ⁷"If," I ask, "the wife has been divorced, she repents and desires to return to her husband, is he to take her back?" ⁸"Yes," he answers. "If the husband does not take her back, he sins and brings condemnation on himself. It is necessary, you see, to welcome the sinner who repents; however, is it not necessary to do that repeatedly, for to the servants of God there is but one chance to repent. As a consequence, the husband should not remarry in order to allow for the repentance of his wife. This course of action applies to both husband and wife. ⁹Not only does a man commit adultery when he defiles his body, but if he acts as the pagans do, he is also guilty of adultery. If, then, someone persists in those practices, and does not repent, separate from him and do not live with him. Otherwise, you participate in his sin. ¹⁰For this reason, you are admonished to live as a single person, whether husband or wife, since in such cases repentance is always possible. ¹¹I am not providing the opportunity," he continues, "for anyone to commit an adulterous act, but so the one who has sinned can sin no more. For previous sins, there is someone who can provide healing. For that one has the power to achieve anything."

Hermas *Mandate* 4.1.1–11

agreed does not go back to Jesus.[14] Absolute prohibition is more in line with the tenor of his other injunctions. The sweeping

14. Matt 19:9

injunction, if original with Jesus, challenges the legitimacy of divorce, and thus the primacy of reproduction in marriage. That represents a radical departure from the tribal mentality.

Jesus may have challenged the tradition at another point. Matthew reports him as saying,

---

Love Your Enemies

From Q Matthew and Luke have taken the complex in which the admonition is embedded but have edited and arranged in different ways. We have taken Matthew's version as the basis, since it appears to have been little altered from the Q text. Luke, on the other hand, has enlarged the complex, rearranging the elements and adding others (omitted in the parallel columns below). We have matched Luke's components to those of Matthew's to simplify matters; the order does not materially affect the meaning.

[44]But I tell you:

Love your enemies

and pray for your persecutors.

[45]You'll then become children of your Father in the heavens.

<God> causes the sun to rise on both the bad and the good, and sends rain on both the just and the unjust.

[46]Tell me, if you love those who love you, why should you be commended for that?

Even the toll collectors do as much, don't they?

[47]And if you greet only your friends, what have you done that is exceptional?

Even the pagans do as much, don't they?

[48]To sum up, you are to be as liberal in your love as your heavenly Father is.

Matt 5:44–48

There are castrated men who were born that way, and there are castrated men who were castrated by others, and there are castrated men who castrated themselves because of Heaven's imperial rule.[15]

15. Matt 19:12

---

[27]But to you who listen I say,
love your enemies,
do favors for those who hate you,
[28]*bless those who curse you,*
pray for your those who abuse you.
[35]and you'll be children of the Most High.

As you know, the Most High is generous to the ungrateful and the wicked.

[32]If you love those who love you, what merit is there in that?

After all, even sinners love those who love them.

[33]And if you do good to those who do good to you, what merit is there in that?

After all, even sinners do as much.

[36]Be compassionate in the way your Father is compassionate.

Luke 6:27–29, 35,32–33,36

Only two observations are required. First, Luke appears to have expanded the initial admonition by inserting two additional clauses (vv. 27b, 28a). Second, Luke's language tends to be more generalized. Matthew, on the other hand, retains very concrete and specific images, such as toll collectors and pagans rather than sinners. Concrete images from the everyday world are characteristic of Jesus' language.

Critical scholars have tended to interpret this saying as an attempt on the part of the early Christian community to accommodate a trend toward asceticism. And that may indeed be its origin. However, it is also possible to understand it as a radical departure from the male-dominated, patriarchal society. In that society, male virility and parenthood were the fundamental norms. The true Israel consisted of males who were capable of fathering children. Priests and Levites had to meet this requirement to be eligible for office. Eunuchs, including males born without testicles, could not be counted among genuine Judeans and thus did not qualify for temple service. If this saying goes back to Jesus, he may have been undermining another tribal tradition and attempting to restore a marginal group of males to full status in the human community.

In any case, Jesus himself probably did not marry. His itinerant lifestyle could not accommodate wife and family, and that may be the reason some of his early followers, such as Paul of Tarsus, imitated him in refusing to marry.[16] Moreover, he taught his disciples to abandon family obligations, to give no thought for food and clothing, to sell their possessions and give the proceeds to the poor. He advised them to ignore obligations to parents and to forsake the patriarchal structure of the extended family, as we have already noted. And, to top it off, he seems to have deserted his own mother and siblings.

Jesus perceived that his world—the received or default world—was coming to an end, not in an apocalyptic conflagration, but in a social transformation. That world did end abruptly and literally in 66–70 C.E. when the Romans destroyed Jerusalem. Yet the social transformation had only begun. It was to play itself out over the next two millennia and more.

---

16. Cf. this passage from Paul (1 Cor 7:10–11): My instructions to those who are married — it is not I but the Lord—that wives should not separate from their husbands. But if they do separate, they are to remain single or else to be reconciled with their husbands. And husbands should not divorce their wives.

Once the tribe is relieved of the pressure to reproduce, once the future of the tribe does not depend on being more prolific than other tribes, or one family more prolific than other families, then the question becomes: What is the function of sex? If sex is not exclusively for reproduction, then what is it for?

This issue has been made acute in modern times by separating conception from sex by various means of contraception or abortion, and, more recently, by disconnecting sex from conception by means of artificial insemination. Sex has become virtually a free commodity, unattached to other human functions. Yet the church, especially the Roman church, has continued to demonize sex by clinging to the tribal mentality and insisting that the sole function of sex is reproduction. According to Augustine, the fall in the garden of Eden came to be understood as a fall into sexuality, which means that all sex is evil, and can be tolerated only by virtue of its necessity to propagate the race. These developments have gone to seed in the modern American slogan, "If you play, you must pay!" It is a truly sick notion that sexual intercourse without the intent to produce a child deserves punishment and the punishment is an unwanted child. And now the American Catholic Bishops, invoking some Augustinian logic, have banned tubal ligations and vasectomies in Catholic hospitals, along with abortions. Bishops in South Africa have even gone so far as to ban the use of condoms – even to prevent the spread of AIDS. It is incredible how inverted theological logic drives such insane conclusions. In retrospect, we see all the more clearly how radical and alien to ecclesiastical behavior the vision of Jesus really was.

Kinship

Hating One's Family (1)

If you come to me and do not hate your own father and mother and wife and children and brothers and sisters – yes, even your own life – you're no disciple of mine. [27]Unless you carry your own cross and come along with me – you're no disciple of mine.

Sources: Q, Thomas • Luke 14:26–27

Hating One's Family (2)

Jesus said, "Whoever does not hate father and mother cannot be my disciple, [2]and whoever does not hate brothers and sisters, and carry the cross as I do, will not be worthy of me."

Sources: Q, Thomas • Thom 55:1–2

True Relatives

Then his mother and his brothers arrive. While still outside, they send in and ask for him. [32]A crowd was sitting around him, and they say to him, "Look, your mother and your brothers and sisters are outside looking for you."

[33]In response he says to them: "My mother and brothers – who ever are they?

[34]And looking right at those seated around him in a circle, he says, "Here are my mother and my brothers. [35]Whoever does God's will, that's my brother and sister and mother!"

Source: Mark • Mark 3:31–35

Kinship

Hate your family

The aphorism, "love your enemies," is perhaps the most radical in the Jesus repertoire. The next most radical saying admonishes followers to "hate your family." It is perhaps the harshest of all the authentic Jesus sayings because it attacks the basic kinship codes that govern the structure of the family unit.

> If you come to me
> and do not hate your own father and mother
> and wife and children
> and brothers and sisters
> – yes, even your own life –
> you're no disciple of mine.
> Unless you carry your own cross
> and come along with me –
> you're no disciple of mine.[1]

This saying very likely originates with Jesus because it is harsh – the early community would not have invented something so cutting – and because it appears in two independent sources.

Matthew and Luke have taken the saying from the Sayings Gospel Q, so we have two witnesses to the Q source. (Luke's version is given above.) In addition, the saying is preserved in two forms in Thomas.

By comparing the sequence in Matthew and Thomas with that in Luke, it is possible to reconstruct the sequence that Matthew and Luke found in Q and even speculate about the original sequence.

1. Luke 14:26–27

Matt 10:37–38

If you love your father and mother more than me,
you're not worthy of me,
and if you love your son or daughter more than me,
you're not worthy of me.
Unless you take your cross
and come along with me,
you're not worthy of me.

Thom 55:1–2

Whoever does not hate father and mother
cannot be my disciple,
and whoever does not hate brothers and sisters,

and carry the cross as I do,

will not be worthy of me.

Thomas 101

Whoever does not hate father and mother as I do
cannot be my disciple,
and whoever does not love father and mother as I do
cannot be my disciple.
For my mother [. . .], but my true [mother] gave me life.

In its form in Q it probably consisted of three couplets:

Unless you hate your father and mother
you're no disciple of mine.
Unless you hate your brothers and sisters,
you're no disciple of mine.
Unless you carry your cross
and come along with me,
you're no disciple of mine.

All three gospels have the three basic elements: father and
mother, brother and sister, cross. The proposed Q text simply
takes those three elements and arranges them in parallel couplets.
Luke has apparently expanded the family to include wife and chil-

dren, and added the clause about hating life. Since these are not reflected in either Matthew or Thomas, they are probably Luke's additions.

Thomas 55, on the other hand, has collapsed the second (brother and sister) and third (cross) elements into one. Further,

True Relatives

We are dependent on Mark and Thomas for the anecdote about Jesus' relation to his mother and siblings. Matthew and Luke copy from and revise Mark. The Gospel of The Ebionites probably draws on all three synoptic gospels, so it is not an independent source. All our sources confirm the basic structure of the story: Jesus' family come to take him home but can't get to him because of the crowd; Jesus proclaims that those who do his Father's will are his true relatives.

> Then his mother and his brothers arrive. While still outside, they send in and ask for him. A crowd was sitting around him, and they say to him, "Look, your mother and your brothers and sisters are outside looking for you."
> In response he says to them: "My mother and brothers – who ever are they?"
> And looking right at those seated around him in a circle, he says, "Here are my mother and my brothers. Whoever does God's will, that's my brother and sister and mother!"
> Mark 3:31–35

> While he was still speaking to the crowds, his mother and brothers showed up outside; they had come to speak to him. Someone said to him, "Look, your mother and your brothers are outside wanting to speak to you."
> In response he said to the one speaking to him, "My mother

Thomas had added the startling phrase "as I do," suggesting that Jesus was calling on his followers to imitate him in relation to family and siblings and willingness to suffer persecution.

Thomas 101 utilizes only the first couplet and then continues with gnostic commentary on that couplet.

---

and my brothers – who ever are they?" And he pointed to his disciples and said, "Here are my mother and my brothers. For whoever does the will of my Father in heaven, that's my brother and sister and mother."
Matt 12:46–50

Then his mother and his brothers came to see him, but they could not reach him because of the crowd. When he was told, "Your mother and your brothers are outside and want to see you," he replied to them, "My mother and my brothers are those who listen to God's message and do it."
Luke 8:19–21

The disciples said to him, "Your brothers and your mother are standing outside."
He said to them, "Those here who do what my Father wants are my brothers and my mother. They are the ones who will enter my Father's domain."
Thom 99:2–3

They deny that he was human, I suppose because of what the Savior said when it was reported to him:

"Look, your mother and your brothers are outside."

"My mother and brothers – who ever are they?" [3]And he pointed to his disciples and said, "These are my brothers and mother and sisters, [4]those who do the will of my Father."
GEbi 5

Most scholars are inclined to the view that the reference to the cross must reflect the Christian view of Jesus' death and therefore cannot be attributed to Jesus. (We cannot assume that Jesus anticipated the kind of death he would die and how that death would be understood.) At the same time, some scholars have argued that "cross" here is a metaphor for the kind of persecution and suffering in store for those who forsake family and become part of the Jesus movement. Its presence in Thomas is a strong argument in support of that view, since Thomas otherwise has no interest in the death of Jesus. Possible allusions to the death of Jesus in Thom 65/66 and 104:3 are weak at best. Despite its questionable authenticity, the fourth beatitude may reflect Jesus' anticipation of some sort of persecution.

> Congratulations to you when they denounce you
> and persecute you
> and spread malicious gossip about you
> because of me[2].

We have reason to think that Jesus and his followers may have been the butt of considerable criticism (a glutton and a drunk, a crony of toll collectors and sinners) and the object of persecution (perhaps on the part of Herod Antipas). The fourth beatitude may thus reproduce the memory of earlier harassment, now being intensified at the time the gospels were being composed. (It is necessary to entertain the possibility of reading every text at two or three levels: Jesus, the early Jesus movement, the community of the evangelists.)

This saying about hating mother and father is about another kind of boundary – blood and family. In another saying, Jesus advises one potential follower to forsake the burial rites normally due his parent and take up his "cross" without delay. Kinship in God's Domain apparently transcends blood and marital relationships. How are we to understand this radical departure from traditional kinship codes?

In Israel, the extended family unit lived in a compound house

2. Matt 5:11

consisting of several rooms arranged around a courtyard, with sleeping quarters on the second floor. When a son of the family married, he brought his bride to his "father's house" to live; a daughter was taken to the house of her husband's father. Such houses have been unearthed in excavations and are termed "the four-room house," although the number four is a misnomer since such houses normally consisted of more than four rooms. The extended family might consist of three or four generations and run to as many as twenty people.

Jesus was probably thinking of such an extended family, living in a complex like the one just described, presided over by an aging patriarch who made life and death decisions for everyone in the family. In the Mediterranean world, the patriarch had virtually unlimited power in the family; there was no escape from his pronouncements. A father could sentence his own son to death, or he could have a girl baby exposed. The disposition of the inheritance was subject to his discretion (note the dispersal of the patrimony in the parable of the prodigal). Children remained under the patriarch's authority until marriage in the case of daughters, or until the death of the father in the case of sons. Under such circumstances, Jesus might well have indicated that his followers must break their ties with the family enclave in order to be open to the radically new way of relating to God's domain. In such a social context, Jesus' harsh dicta about the family enclave thus makes eminent sense, especially if we do not insist that he meant "hate" literally.

Almost from the beginning, Christians have been inclined to ignore this saying or remodel it. Matthew has simply turned the saying around to make it more acceptable to polite society. His version reads: "If you love your father and mother more than me, . . . you're not worthy of me."[3] His community did not like, or did not understand, the radical demand in its original form. This is another example of the way in which the radical sayings of Jesus were softened and blunted as the tradition developed.

The contrast between the love of enemies and the hatred of

3. Matt 10:37

family is striking. The one blows away the tribal boundary, the other demolishes family ties. Kinship in the realm of God rearranges the social map of the community.

True relatives

The saying about hating father and mother goes together with an anecdote told about Jesus in the synoptics and Thomas. In the story Jesus' relatives come to get him because they think him mad. When informed of their presence, Jesus turns to his audience and asks, "My mother and my brothers – whoever are they?" He answers his own question with this saying: "Whoever does God's will, that's my brother and sister and mother."[4]

This saying may echo the conflict between Jesus and his immediate relatives. Later, his brother James seems to have changed his mind and joined the Jesus movement, perhaps in an effort to reclaim the legacy of his brother. The saying could also be understood to refer metaphorically to those who accepted him and those who rejected him. We cannot be sure. However, in the context of "love your enemies" and "hate your father and mother," we can probably attribute it to Jesus.

There lurks behind this complex the suspicion that Jesus was estranged from his family during much or all of his public life. That makes it very likely that the birth and childhood stories are fictions pure and simple, looking back as they then would from the distance of family reconciliation following the death of Jesus and shaped by the influence of other contemporary stories of precocious heroes.

4. Mark 3:35

Flora & Fauna

God & Birds

Take a look at the birds of the sky: they don't plant or harvest or gather into barns. Yet your heavenly Father feeds them.

Source Q • Matt 6:26

God & Lilies

Notice how the wild lilies grow: They don't slave and they never spin. Yet let me tell you, even Solomon at the height of his glory was never decked out like one of them.

Source Q • Matt 6:28–29

God & Sparrows (1)

What do sparrows cost? A dime a dozen? Yet not one of them is overlooked by God.

Source: Q • Luke 12:6

God & Sparrows (2)

What do sparrows cost? A penny apiece? Yet not one of them will fall to the earth without the consent of your Father.

Source Q • Matt 10:29

God & Grass

If God dresses the grass in the field, which is here today and tomorrow is tossed into the oven, it is surely more likely that God cares for you, you who don't take anything for granted!

Source Q • Luke 12:28

God & Hair

In fact, even the hairs of your head have been counted.

Source Q • Luke 12:7 a

Sun & Rain

The Father causes the sun to rise on both the bad and the good, and sends rain on both the just and the unjust.

Source Q • Matt 5:45b

The Sower

Listen to this! This sower went out to sow. [4]While he was sowing, some seed fell along the path, and the birds came and ate it up. [5]Other seed fell on rocky ground where there wasn't much soil, and it came up right away because the soil had no depth. [6]But when the sun came up it was scorched, and because it had no root it withered. [7]Still other seed fell among thorns, and the thorns came up and choked it, so that it produced no fruit. [8]Finally, some seed fell on good earth and started producing fruit. The seed sprouted and grew: one part had a yield of thirty, another part sixty, and a third part one hundred.

Source: Mark • Mark 4:3–8

Seed & Harvest

God's imperial rule is like this: Suppose someone sows seed on the ground, [27]and goes to bed and gets up day after day, and the seed sprouts and matures, although the sower is unaware of it. [28]The earth produces fruit on its own, first a shoot, then a head, then mature grain on the head. [29]But when the grain ripens, all of a sudden <that farmer> sends for the sickle, because it's harvest time.

Source: Mark • Mark 4:26–29

Mustard Seed

The disciples said to Jesus, "Tell us what Heaven's imperial rule is like."

[2]He said to them,

"It's like a mustard seed. [3]It's the smallest of all seeds, [4]but when it falls on prepared soil, it produces a large branch and becomes a shelter for birds of the sky."

Sources: Thomas, Mark, Q • Thom 20:2–4

Leaven

What does God's imperial rule remind me of? [21]It is like leaven that a woman took and concealed in fifty pounds of flour until it was all leavened.

Sources: Q, Thomas • Luke 13:20–21

Foxes & Birds

As they were going along the road, someone said to him, "I'll follow you wherever you go."

[58]And Jesus said to him, "Foxes have dens, and birds of the sky have nests; but this mother's son has nowhere to rest his head."

Sources: Q, Thomas • Luke 9:57–58

Lost Sheep

Is there any one of you who owns a hundred sheep and has one stray off, who wouldn't leave the ninety-nine in the wilderness, and go after the one that got lost until he finds it? [5]And when he finds it, he lifts it up on his shoulders, happy. [6]Once he gets home, he invites his friends and his neighbors over, and says to them, "Celebrate with me, because I have found my lost sheep."

Sources: Q, Thomas • Luke 15:4–6

Precious Pearl

The Father's imperial rule is like a merchant who had a supply of merchandise and then found a pearl. [2]That merchant was prudent; he sold the merchandise and bought the single pearl for himself.

Sources: Thomas, Matthew • Thom 76:1–2

Needle's Eye

And again I tell you, it's easier for a camel to squeeze through a needle's eye than for a wealthy person to get into God's domain.

Source: Mark • Matt 19:24

Tree & Fruit

You'll know who they are by what they produce. Since when do people pick grapes from thorns or figs from thistles? [17]Every healthy tree produces choice fruit, but the rotten tree produces spoiled fruit. [18]A healthy tree cannot produce spoiled fruit, any more than a rotten tree can produce choice fruit. [19]Every tree that does not produce choice fruit gets cut down and tossed on the fire. [20]Remember, you'll know who they are by what they produce.

Sources: Q, Thomas • Matt 7:16–20

Sly as a Snake

Look, I'm sending you out like sheep to a pack of wolves. Therefore you must be as sly as a snake and as simple as a dove.

Sources: Matthew, Thomas • Matt 10:16

Wine & Wineskins

Nobody drinks aged wine and immediately wants to drink young wine. [4]Young wine is not poured into old wineskins, or they might break, and aged wine is not poured into a new wineskin, or it might spoil. [5]And old patch is not sewn onto a new garment, since it would create a tear.

Sources: Mark, Thomas, common lore • Thom 47:3–5

Flora & Fauna

The Realm where God reigns encompasses the animal and plant world as well as the human world. Consider the birds, Jesus suggests:

> They don't plant or harvest,
> or gather into barns.
> Yet your heavenly Father feeds them.[1]

When advising his followers not to be concerned about clothing, he reminds them of the lilies of growing wild in the field:

> Notice how the wild lilies grow:
> They don't slave and they never spin.
> Yet let me tell you,
> even Solomon at the height of his glory
> was never decked out lie one of them.[2]

The sparrows come under the direct surveillance of the Father, according to Jesus. What are sparrows worth, he asks rhetorically, thinking of what it costs to buy them in the temple market:

> What do sparrows cost?
> A dime a dozen?
> Yet not one of them is overlooked by God.[3]

Or, as Matthew editorializes:

> Yet not one of them will fall to the earth without the consent of your Father.[4]

1. Matt 6:26
2. Matt 6:28–29

3. Luke 12:6
4. Matt 10:29

Jesus allows that God adorns the grass of the field, which is here today and tomorrow is tossed into an oven.[5] That is attention to detail at the lowest level. Care for the grass is perhaps commensurate with counting the hairs on the human head.[6]

The divine concern for birds and flowers goes together with the divine compassion in causing the sun to shine and the rain to fall:

The Father causes the sun to rise on both the bad and the good, and sends rain on both the just and the unjust.[7]

Matthew has taken this saying from the Sayings Gospel Q, in all probability.

That Jesus was especially conscious of the natural world around him is indicated by the numerous symbols and analogies he takes from that world.

Seed and soils are the subject matter of the parable of the sower;[8] seed and harvest forms the content of another parable.[9] The mustard seed and the bush that produces it are the primary symbols in one of Jesus' most important parables.[10] Jesus takes a major metaphor from the kitchen when he speaks of a woman baking bread.[11] The vineyard is the setting for another of Jesus' parables.[12] While those who labor in the vineyard are the focus, the background is again the world of agriculture and nature. A similar example of agricultural imagery is the parable of the leased vineyard, one which suffered modification as the tradition was passed on.[13]

In his aphorisms, he compares himself to foxes with their dens and birds with their nests;[14] he tells a story about a lost sheep,[15] about precious pearls,[16] about camels squeezing through a needle's eye,[17] and about healthy and rotten trees.[18] He reasons that people do not pick grapes from thorns, or figs from thistles.[19]

5. Luke 12:28
6. Luke 12:7
7. Matt 6:45
8. Mark 4:3–8
9. Mark 4:26–29
10. Thom 20:2–4
11. Luke 13:20–21
12. Matt 20:1–15
13. Thom 65:1–7
14. Luke 9:57–58
15. Luke 15:4–6
16. Thom 76:1–2
17. Matt 19:24
18. Matt 7:17
19. Matt 7:16

When sending his disciples out on a journey, he advises them, "Be as sly as a snake and simple as a dove."[20]

He suggests that no one wants young wine when aged wine is available.[21] He observes that young wine is not stored in old wineskins, and mature wine is not entrusted to new wineskins, since the former might break and the latter spoil.[22] Nor is an old patch is sewn onto a new garment, since a tear would result when the garment shrinks.[23]

Repeated allusions to the natural world around him indicate that Jesus was acutely aware of that world. The earthiness of his comparisons betokens an intimate relation to vineyards, wine and wineskins, birds and foxes, planting and harvest. There can be little doubt that Jesus embraced the non-human world in his vision of God's domain. To be sure, Jesus values the human world above the natural world, but he includes the flora and fauna within the realm of God's providence, within the boundaries of God's domain.

20. Matt 10:16
21. Thom 47:3
22. Thom 47:4
23. Thom 47:5

Values Are Counterintuitive

Care for the Dead

Leave the dead to bury their own dead.

Source: Q • Luke 9:60

First & Last

The last will be first and the first last.

Sources: Mark, Q, Thomas • Matt 20:16

Number One as Servant

If any of you wants to be 'number one,' you have to be last of all and servant of all!

Source: Mark • Mark 9:35

Saving One's Life

Whoever tries to hang on to life will forfeit it, but whoever forfeits life will preserve it.

Sources: Q, Mark, John • Luke 17:33

Vineyard Laborers

For Heaven's imperial rule is like a proprietor who went out the first thing in the morning to hire workers for his vineyard. [2]After agreeing with the workers for a silver coin a day he sent them into his vineyard.

[3]And coming out around nine A.M. he saw others loitering in the marketplace [4]and he said to them, "You go into the vineyard too, and I'll pay you whatever is fair." [5]So they went.

Around noon he went out again, and at three P.M. he repeated the process. [6]About five P.M. he went out and found others loitering about and says to them, "Why did you stand around here idle the whole day?"

[7]They reply, "Because no one hired us."

He tells them, "You go into the vineyard as well."

[8]When evening came the owner of the vineyard tells his

foreman: "Call the workers and pay them their wages starting with those hired last and ending with those hired first."

[9]Those hired at five P.M. came up and received a silver coin each. [10]Those hired first approached thinking they would receive more. But they also got a silver coin apiece. [11]They took it and began to grumble against the proprietor: [12]"These guys hired last worked only an hour but you have made them equal to us who did most of the work during the heat of the day."

[13]In response he said to one of them, "Look, pal, did I wrong you? You did agree with me for a silver coin, didn't you? [14]Take your wage and get out! I intend to treat the one hired last the same way I treat you. [15]Is there some law forbidding me to do as I please with my money? Or is your eye filled with envy because I am generous?"

Source: Matthew • Matt 20:1–15

Shrewd Manager

There was this rich man whose manager had been accused of squandering his master's property. [2]He called him in and said, "What's this I hear about you? Let's have an audit of your management, because your job is being terminated."

[3]Then the manager said to himself, "What am I going to do? My master is firing me. I'm not able to dig ditches and I'm ashamed to beg. [4]I've got it! I know what I'll do so doors will open for me when I'm removed from management."

[5]So he called in each of his master's debtors. He said to the first, "How much do you owe my master?"

[6]He said, "Five hundred gallons of olive oil."

And he said to him, "Here is your invoice; sit down right now and make it two hundred and fifty."

[7]Then he said to another, "And how much do you owe?"

He said, "A thousand bushels of wheat."

He says to him, "Here is your invoice; make it eight hundred."

[8]The master praised the dishonest manager because he had acted shrewdly.

Source: Luke • Luke 16:1–8a

Values Are Counterintuitive

Jesus' vision of the domain of God is counterintuitive. The divine domain runs counter to recipe knowledge. The reign of God cannot be directly perceived. He suggests that his Father's domain is hidden— a utopia, if you will. (A utopia is literally "no place.") At the same time, God's realm is a pantopia; it is everywhere. It is both no place and yet everywhere. He advocates celebrating the intangible: the hungry, he assures, them, will have a feast; those in mourning will have a good laugh. Only outcasts and outsiders are insiders. He advocates loving enemies but hating families. Like the room in Alice's looking glass, things in God's domain run the other way around.

He underscores this dyslexic arrangement in a series of aphorisms that trumpet reversals.

> The last will be first and the first last.[1]

He advises his followers, those who have aspirations for positions of leadership and power,

> If any of you wants to be 'number one,' you
> have to be last of all and servant of all.[2]

And the most disconcerting reversal of them all concerns life:

> Whoever tries to hang on to life will forfeit it,
> but whoever forfeits life will preserve it.[3]

The impulse to care appropriately for the dead, especially relatives, is attacked in another admonition,

> Leave the dead to bury their own dead.[4]

1. Matt 20:16
2. Mark 9:35
3. Luke 17:33
4. Luke 9:60

Into this harsh saying he has loaded the accusation that many living are in fact dead. These aphorisms undermine direct, rational, received knowledge and custom at their foundations.

In his parables, too, he upsets conventions. Equal pay for equal work is a rule to which most human beings subscribe. But in the parable of the Vineyard Laborers, he has the owner pay those who worked only one hour the same wage as those who toiled the entire day. In God's domain, all we can rely on is the certainty that things will not be what we expect.

The rich employer fires the manager who has been squandering his property. The shrewd manager settles accounts with the employer's debtors for fifty cents on the dollar, thus making friends for himself. But, then, to everyone's surprise, the employer commends the manager for his shrewdness. In God's domain, we are unable to predict the outcome. The resolution is always unexpected, just as God's magnanimity always comes as a surprise.

The counterintuitive nature of God's rule is perpetual: whenever we become certain that we know what it is, we can be even more certain that it is not that. That requires living without reservation into a completely open future.

New Symbols
Parody the Old

Leaven

What does God's imperial rule remind me of? [21]It is like leaven that a woman took and concealed in fifty pounds of flour until it was all leavened.

Sources: Q, Thomas • Luke 13:20–21

Mustard Seed

The disciples said to Jesus, "Tell us what Heaven's imperial rule is like." [2]He said to them,

"It's like a mustard seed. [3]It's the smallest of all seeds, [4]but when it falls on prepared soil, it produces a large plant and becomes a shelter for birds of the sky."

Sources: Thomas, Mark, Q • Thom 20:2–4

Empty Jar

Jesus said, "The [Father's] imperial rule is like a woman who was carrying a [jar] full of meal. [2]While she was walking along [a] distant road, the handle of the jar broke and the meal spilled behind her [along] the road. [3]She didn't know it; she hadn't noticed a problem. [4]When she reached her house, she put the jar down and discovered that it was empty."

Source: Thomas • Thom 97:1–4

New Symbols
Parody the Old

The frustration and reversal of ordinary expectations, the hidden character of God's presence, and the celebration that attends the recognition and acknowledgement of these features is summed up in the parable of the leaven. At the same time, this parable erodes the connection of unleavened bread with hospitality and the sacred.

The leaven is a one-sentence picture parable that may be translated this way:

> God's domain may be compared to *leaven* which a woman took and *concealed* in *fifty pounds of flour* until it was all leavened.[1]

The key terms here are leaven, concealed, and fifty pounds of flour.

Nomads in the biblical period normally ate unleavened bread. And they served unleavened or flat bread (similar to what we know as pita bread) on occasions of special hospitality. When two angels visited Lot in Sodom, he entertained them with a feast, the principal ingredient of which was unleavened bread.[2] It was the lack of hospitality that may have lead to the destruction of Sodom and Gomorrah. Abraham probably served unleavened bread to the three angels when they visited him at the Oaks of Mamre.[3] Although the preparations he and Sarah made were elaborate, he may not have been unaware of who the three figures were; if not, he was merely fulfilling the obligations of hospitality.

---

1. Luke 13:21
2. Gen 19:1–3

3. Gen 18:1–8

On the other hand, a grain offering in the temple consisted of unleavened cakes or unleavened wafers.[4] During Passover, the Israelites were to eat unleavened bread for seven days: "On the first day you are to remove leaven from your houses. Whoever eats leavened bread from the first day to the seventh is to be exiled from Israel."[5] In later rabbinic literature, leaven is regarded as corrupting and therefore evil. Paul of Tarsus apparently shared this view of leaven:

The fact that you are proud of this affair is not good. Don't you know that a little bit of leaven affects the whole batch of dough? Clean out the old leaven so that you can be a fresh batch of dough, because spiritually you really are uncontaminated by the old leaven. Since Christ, our Passover lamb, so to speak, has been sacrificed, we should celebrate the feast of our liberation not with the leaven of vice and base behavior, but with the unleavened bread of integrity and truth.[6]

Jesus apparently does not share the negative attitude toward leaven. On the contrary, he employs leaven as a symbol of God's realm, thus undermining the old associations. The use of leaven in a positive sense inverts the locus of the sacred: where the sacred is, no leaven is permitted. In contrast, Jesus deliberately associates leaven with the divine realm.

In the parable, the woman *conceals* the yeast in flour: That is a hint that the presence of God's imperial rule is not overtly discernible. God's domain is a hidden or invisible realm.

And fifty pounds of flour is what was required for Abraham's experience at the oaks of Mamre when visited by the angels: it is the amount needed to celebrate an epiphany.

Here in the space of just a few words Jesus clusters a number of features of the domain of God as he imagines it. The fellows of the Jesus Seminar decided that this parable was Jesus at his parsimonious and metaphorical best.[7]

---

4. Lev 2:4–6
5. Exod 12:15

6. 1 Cor 5:6–8 SV
7. *The Five Gospels*, p. 195.

In a similar vein, the parable of the mustard seed is a parody of the mighty cedar of Lebanon employed by Ezekiel to symbolize the kingdom of David and Solomon. In his vision, Ezekiel envisions Yahweh taking a tender twig from the lofty heights of the noble cedar and planting it on a mountain in Israel.[8] From that twig will grow a mighty tree that will become a haven for every kind of bird. This tree is not a real tree; it is an apocalyptic tree, under which all humankind will eventually gather.

The mighty cedar symbolizes the secular powers of the earth. The cedar of Israel will exceed all the other trees of the forest in majesty and grandeur. That will demonstrate that Yahweh will exalt the lowly tree but humble the mighty tree.

God's realm, in contrast, may be compared to a lowly, pesky weed that attracts birds who feed on its seed. The parable of the mustard seed is a parody of Ezekiel's mighty cedar, a symbol also utilized in Daniel.[9] The reign of God is nothing more ominous than the perennial mustard that grows only to bush size. It is modest in its pretensions, yet it serves as food and shelter for the birds.

The parable of the empty jar, found only in Thomas, is a lampoon of the story of Elijah and the widow of Zarephath.[10] The widow has a jar containing only a handful of meal for her son and herself during a famine. Nevertheless, she is told to feed Elijah from the little that she has. She heeds the instructions of Yahweh and the meal is not depleted by her generosity. Jesus reverses the image: the jar of meal is not miraculously replenished, but is accidentally emptied of its contents. Apparently many in God's domain are to go hungry.

These three parables subvert the old symbols. They poke fun at the ancient triumphalist traditions. The sacred is relocated in the secular; the ephemeral mustard weed dwarfs the cedars of Lebanon; and supply of food in the kingdom is not abundant.

8. Ezek 17:22–24   10. 1 Kgs 17:8–16
9. Dan 4:4–18

Subverting the System

10.

The Other Cheek

When someone slaps you on the right cheek, turn the other as well.

Source: Q • Matt 5:39

Coat & Shirt

If someone sues you for your coat, give him the shirt off your back to go with it.

Source: Q • Matt 5:40

Second Mile

When anyone conscripts you for one mile, go along two.

Source: Q • Matt 5:41

Lend Without Return

If you have money, don't lend it at interest. Rather, give it to someone from whom you won't get it back.

Sources: Thomas, Q • Thom 95:1–2

Give to Beggars

Give to everyone who begs from you.

Source: Q • Matt 5:42a

Before the Judge

When you are about to appear with your opponent before the magistrate, do your best to settle with him on the way, or else he might drag you up before the judge, and the judge turn your over to the jailer, and the jailer throw you in prison. [59]I tell you, you'll never get out of there until you've paid your last red cent.

Source: Q • Luke 12:58–59

Subverting
the System

This group of aphorisms indicates Jesus wanted to subvert the system, to undermine the social, political, and economic way of doing things. Together these sayings probably do not constitute the mandate for a social revolution, but they do hint that Jesus is intent on undermining the status quo.

The first of these, taken from Q, is frequently misinterpreted. In the version preserved by Luke it reads:

When someone slaps you on the right cheek,
turn the other as well.[1]

It has been understood to order victims of violence to submit to further violence. It has been interpreted to apply to battered women who are commanded to submit to those who abuse them. It has been explained as the ethical norm to be completely pacifistic in response to aggression.

The misunderstanding, as Walter Wink has explained, arises out of the nature of the slap or the cuff on the cheek. Luke specifies the right cheek as the locus of the blow (Matthew has omitted that important detail). A fist to the face would normally land on the left cheek were the assailant right-handed. The left hand was not normally used for combative purposes in Mediterranean society. It was reserved for less seemly functions, such as toilet hygiene. In the Qumran community, for example, a gesture with the left hand was punishable by an expulsion from the community for ten days, coupled with an act of penance. The situation Jesus has in mind here is one in which a superior slaps a supposed inferior with the back of the hand. It is the appropriate gesture of

1. Luke 5:39

96

a Roman to a Jew, of a master to a slave, of husband to wife, of
parent to child. It is intended to send a social message: get back
in your place; remember who you are; be subservient.

The response Jesus proposes is subversive: By offering the
other cheek you send an equally powerful message. It is an act of
defiance. It is a statement that proclaims the parity of the victim:
'I am not your inferior. I have my rights. I am a human being. I
refuse to be treated like an inferior specimen of the human race.'
The aggressor is now at a loss. The backhanded blow cannot be
repeated on the left cheek. And to be reduced to fisticuffs would
mean to acknowledge the equality of the two parties.

Jesus counsels against passive submission. He does not recom-
mend returning violence for violence, but neither does he suggest that victims resign themselves to their fate. Emancipation
begins with this simple yet effective act of resistance to oppression. It is well to remember that in Roman society such an act of
defiance might result in the death of the victim. Masters held the
right of life or death over slaves, as did fathers over children, and
Romans over non-Romans. To turn the other cheek is a bold step
in undermining the system.

The second of these, also taken from Q, needs some revision
since both Matthew and Luke seem to have garbled it. The version preserved by the Didache, a second century manual, appears
to follow Matthew. The three versions may be readily compared
in this table:

Luke 6:29b

If someone takes away your coat,
don't prevent that person from taking your shirt along with it.

Matt 5:40

If someone sues you for your shirt,
give him your coat to go with it.

Did 1:4

If anyone takes your shirt,
give that person your coat also.

Coat and shirt are confusing terms relative to the typical garments worn in Jesus' day. His was a two-garment society. People wore an undergarment, here termed a "shirt," and they wore an outer garment when the weather or occasion required it. We have translated that term as "coat," although "cloak" might have been a better term.

In financial transactions, collateral normally consisted of sheep or goats, or, if the borrower was wealthy enough, land. But when such transactions involved peasants with little or no wealth, the coat or outer garment could be pledged as collateral for a loan. However, there were limitations imposed on the creditor, as indicated by this passage from Deuteronomy:

> If you make your neighbor a loan, a loan of any kind, you must not enter the neighbor's house to take possession of the property pledged as collateral. You are to wait outside, and the person to whom you made the loan will bring the property outside to you. If that person is poor, you must not sleep in the garment given you as collateral. You are to return the cloak to that person before the sun goes down, so that he may sleep in his own cloak and bless you for it. Besides, you will get credit with the Lord your God.[2]

It is a tough banker who takes possession of a cloak as collateral. But the banker was obligated to return the cloak to the owner at sundown, since the borrower needed his cloak to sleep under at night.

Matthew has turned the relation of coat and shirt around. In the case of default, the lender could sue the peasant for pledged collateral, namely, his cloak. A peasant was very unlikely to succeed in winning a reprieve in the courts. Clearly, Jesus has elected to illustrate with an extreme case. He gives this advice: when someone wants to sue you for your cloak, give that person the shirt off your back to go with it. That will bring the system down. Jesus is proposing that the debtor strip naked to expose the injustice of the law. Since nakedness was taboo in Israel, the creditor would be shamed.

2. Deut 24:10–14 (LXX)

The gospels have thus garbled the tradition. Matthew is correct in suggesting that a lawsuit involving default on a loan is involved. Luke has obscured or lost that feature and seems to be thinking of a robbery. But Luke has the order correct: first cloak, then shirt. The Didache unthinkingly follows Matthew's order of garments, but has lost the legal frame of reference. No doubt these variations in the tradition reflect changing social circumstance as the Jesus movement expanded, changed social locations, and matured. The original form of the aphorism is thus:

> If someone sues you for your coat,
> give him the shirt off your back to go with it.[3]

In a two-garment society, that advice meant capitulating by stripping to the buff. There is humor in that suggestion and I cannot imagine that people did not titter when he said it. But it was also serious advice—not only if followed literally, but if one understood his real goal: His suggestion is to subvert the system by refusing to participate in the confiscatory process. Concede, he says, and see what happens.

A third aphorism in the group preserved by Matthew but not found in Luke is the command to go the second mile:

> When anyone conscripts you for one mile,
> go along two.[4]

Whether this saying was part of the Q text is now difficult to determine, although Luke had good reason, in view of his Roman readers, to omit the reference to conscripted service. Since the saying fits nicely with the admonition to turn the other cheek and to relinquish both coat and shirt in undermining the system, it seems appropriate to include it in the authentic Jesus repertoire.

The Roman army marched along Roman roads marked by milestones. Packs were as heavy in those days as they are in ours. Roman soldiers were permitted to conscript natives to help them with their loads, but such portage was limited by military law to

3. Matt 5:40 revised.
4. Matt 5:41

one mile. Centurions in command had the right to enforce the rule, although they might choose not to do so.

Imagine, then, the surprise of the soldier who has reached the first mile marker with his conscripted bearer only to have the native offer to go a second mile. As Walter Wink again points out, he would be in a quandary to accept the offer. To do so might anger his commander, who had to be mindful of native resentment at excessive Roman demands. The offer is designed to expose injustice and servitude but to do so with surprise and humor. Accordingly, one cannot assume these proposals are rules to be rigidly followed, but are creative suggestions intended to assail and erode the system.

Modern interpreters of this set of aphorisms have understood them well when they put them into practice as forms of active non-violent resistance to oppression and evil. Jesus is not advocating nonresistance to injustice; he appears to be engaged in subverting ordinary forms of oppression with humorous but aggressive non-violent acts.

Walter Wink has taught and practiced these ethical guidelines for many years around the globe. Since he has the advantage of *practice* as well as theory, it worth quoting his evaluation of these three admonitions of Jesus:

> Jesus' solution was neither utopian nor apocalyptic. . . .
>
> For three centuries, the early church observed Jesus' command to nonviolence. But nowhere in the early church, to say nothing of the early fathers, do we find statements similar to these in their humor and originality. These sayings are, in fact, so radical, so unprecedented, and so threatening, that it has taken all these centuries just to begin to grasp their implications.[5]

Another set of aphorisms concerns begging and borrowing. The admonition on giving to beggars is derived from Q.

Luke 6:30a
Give to everyone who begs from you.

5. *Engaging the Powers*, p. 184.

Matt 5:42a

Give to the one who begs from you.

In the Roman world, beggars were ubiquitous, as they are in the modern Near East. Taken literally, this admonition would bankrupt the most affluent in a matter of days. Yet, as an itinerant, Jesus understood how important were the laws of hospitality. And he responded to the plight of the poor, especially those without any means of livelihood other than begging. Furthermore, he knew how deep the impulse to charity was in his own tradition. It is not surprising then that he advises those listening to respond positively to every request for a handout.

Of course, we must understand this absolute admonition to have been spoken with tongue in cheek. It is no more to be taken as a rule of law than other of his ethical pronouncements. But it is consonant with his trust ethic: I must trust those I meet along the road to supply my minimal needs, and so you, too, should be ready to help the impoverished with their minimal needs. That fundamental trust informs Jesus' rhetoric and behavior everywhere. The Samaritan responds to the need of the man in the ditch; a neighbor responds to the friend at midnight; and the disciples are taught to ask only for one day's bread at a time. "Give to everyone who begs from you" belongs to that same genre of admonition. It participates in both a literal and metaphorical horizon of meaning.

No less radical is a set of sayings concerning lending and borrowing. This set has also suffered some distortion in transmission. The three forms are exhibited in the chart below.

Luke 6:30b

and when someone takes your things, don't ask for them back.

Matt 5:42b

and don't turn away the one who tries to borrow from you.

Thom 95:1–2

Jesus said, "If you have money, don't lend it at interest. Rather, give it to someone from whom you won't get it back."

The Q saying is best preserved by Matthew: Don't turn away from the one who wants to borrow from you. The form in Thomas, which the Fellows of the Jesus Seminar concluded was closer to the authentic Jesus, is even more radical. It specifies that money should be deliberately lent to those who won't be able to pay it back. Moreover, lending should have no interest attached to it. Advice of this kind is clearly a threat to the system.

The onerous burden of taxes and debt was oppression of the worst kind to the Galilean peasant in Jesus' day. Relief from that oppression had to involve outright grants or interest-free loans. That sounds very utopian. But as we have learned in the modern world, banking practices of just that order have become essential to underdeveloped societies and global stability. Jesus undoubtedly knew that his advice would not, perhaps should not, be taken literally on every occasion; yet he was realist enough to know that some form of assistance was essential to the chronically poor in Galilee.

This group of sayings provides examples of behavior that frustrates the established order. Jesus' advice to settle on the way to the magistrate, which the Seminar took to derive from Jesus, counsels avoiding the system altogether. Settle out of court is his sage advice. Otherwise you will find that you have lost ground, since the system does not favor your cause.

Walter Wink has developed these ideas at length in his trilogy on the powers: *Naming the Powers* (1984); *Unmasking the Powers* (1986); *Engaging the Powers* (1992).

No Room for Demons

House Divided

Every government divided against itself is devastated, and a house divided against a house falls. [18]If Satan is divided against himself – since you claim I drive out demons in Beelzebul's name – how will his domain endure?

Sources: Q, Mark • Luke 11:17–18

Satan's Fall

I was watching Satan fall like lightning from heaven.

Source: Luke • Luke 10:18

Demons by the Finger of God

If I drive out demons in Beelzebul's name, in whose name do your own people drive them out? In that case, they will be your judges. [20]But if by God's finger I drive out demons, then for you God's imperial rule has arrived.

Source: Q • Luke 11:19–20

Jesus Demon Possessed

Many of them [the Judeans] were saying, 'He's out of his mind and crazy. Why pay attention to him? ' [21]Others were saying, 'These aren't the words of someone who is demon-possessed. A demon can't open the eyes of the blind, can it?'

Source: John • John 10:20–21

In League with Satan

Then he goes home, and once again a crowd gathers, so they could not even grab a bite to eat. [21]When his relatives heard about it, they came to get him. (You see, they thought he was out of his mind.) [22]And the scholars who had come down from Jerusalem would say, "He is under the control of Beelzebul" and "He drives out demons in the name of the head demon!" [23]And after calling them over, he would speak to them in riddles: "How can Satan drive out Satan? [24]After all, if a government is divided against itself, that government cannot endure. [25]And if a household is divided against itself, that household won't be able to survive. [26]So if Satan rebels against himself and is divided, he cannot endure but is done for."

Sources: Mark, Q • Mark 3:20–26

Powerful Man

How can someone enter a powerful man's house and steal his possessions, unless he first ties him up? Only then does he loot his house.

Sources: Mark, Q, Thomas • Matt 12:29

True Relatives

Then his mother and his brothers arrive. While still outside, they send in and ask for him. [32]A crowd was sitting around him, and they say to him, "Look, your mother and your brothers and sisters are outside looking for you."

[33]In response he says to them: "My mother and brothers — who ever are they?"

[34]And looking right at those seated around him in a circle, he says, "Here are my mother and my brothers. [35]Whoever does God's will, that's my brother and sister and mother!"

Sources: Mark, Thomas • Mark 3:31–35

No Room
for Demons

As is often the case with visionaries, Jesus' vision reached into some unknown future. He seems to have imagined a time when the heavens would be cleared of the principalities and powers that popular religion in his time believed to control human destiny. He is reported to have observed the fall of Satan from the skies; that would be tantamount to witnessing the end of heavenly demonic powers. Of course, the heavens were not to be cleared of those forces in the minds of most people until after the Enlightenment and rise of the sciences, and then only in the case of the truly literate. Many in the twenty-first century retain the conviction, or perhaps the hope, that astral influences still hover over the destinies of human beings. It would be difficult otherwise to explain the continuing popularity of astrological charts and related phenomena at the checkout stands in supermarkets and drug stores.

In Jesus' case, we are fairly certain that he exorcised what were thought to be demons. We do not know whether he really believed in demons, yet if he thought that the heavens had been swept clean of Satan and the powers, that conviction would indicate that had abandoned the older view. In any case, we are confident that he was accused of being demon-possessed. In the Gospel of John, for example, many Judeans were saying that Jesus was out of his mind – crazy.[1] To be out of one's mind was believed to be the result of demon possession. In Mark's gospel, this story is told about Jesus:

> Then he goes home, and once again a crowd gathers, so they could not even grab a bite to eat. When his relatives heard about it, they came to get him. (You see, they thought

1. John 10:20

he was out of his mind.) And the scholars who had come down from Jerusalem would say, "He is under the control of Beelzebul" and "He drives out demons in the name of the head demon!" [2]

Since Jesus was under the control of Beelzebul, he must be mad, and his ability to drive demons out was connected with that malady.

In his response, however, he turned their logic against them:

> And after calling them over, he would speak to them in riddles:
>
> "How can Satan drive out Satan? After all, if a government is divided against itself, that government cannot endure. And if a household is divided against itself, that household won't be able to survive. So if Satan rebels against himself and is divided, he cannot endure but is done for." [3]

By conceding that he may be in league with Satan, and by admitting that he drives demons out, he concludes, to the consternation of his accusers, that Satan is divided against himself and thus is done for. A household divided against itself is bound to fall.

The complex in Mark and the Sayings Gospel Q contains an additional observation:

> How can someone enter a powerful man's house and steal his possessions, unless he first ties him up? Only then does he loot his house. [4]

Of course, the thief must first disable the powerful one. And so, it becomes plain that Jesus has disabled Satan and his cronies, the demons. So Jesus concludes:

> I was watching Satan fall like lightning from heaven. [5]

This saying is reported to have been uttered in the context of an exorcism, so it may reflect an insight that reaches far into the

2. Mark 3:20–22   4. Matt 12:29
3. Mark 3:23–26   5. Luke 10:18

cultural future: The heavens are no longer home to the principalities and powers; the skies have been swept clean. That observation is linked to another saying concerning the arrival of God's imperial rule:

> But if by God's finger I drive out demons, then for you God's imperial rule has arrived.[6]

Evidently Jesus' mother and siblings shared the common opinion that he was out of his mind. They came to get him, as we observed above, to take him home and out of harm's way. But when their arrival is announced for that purpose, Jesus asks rhetorically:

> My mother and brothers – who ever are they?

Looking at those gathered around, he continues:

> Here are my mother and my brothers. Whoever does God's will, that's my brother and sister and mother![7]

A stinging rebuke to his family. But a powerful glimpse of a world that lay centuries off.

6. Luke 11:20   7. Mark 3:33–35

Rewards Are Intrinsic

Terms of Forgiveness (1)

Forgive and you'll be forgiven.

Source: Q • Luke 6:37c

Terms of Forgiveness (2)

Forgive our debts to the extent we have forgiven those in debt to us.

Source: Q • Matt 6:12

No Merit in Love

If you love those who love you, why should you be commended for that? Even the toll collectors do as much, don't they?

Source: Q • Matt 5:46

Children of the Father

You'll then become children of your Father.

Source: Q • Matt 5:45a

Sun & Rain

God causes the sun to rise on both the bad and the good, and sends rain on both the just and the unjust.

Source: Q • Matt 5:45b

Liberal Love

To sum up, you are to be as liberal in your love as your heavenly Father is.

Source: Q • Matt 5:48

Flaunting Religion in Public

Take care that you don't flaunt your religion in public to be noticed by others. Otherwise, you will have no recognition from your Father in the heavens.

Source: Matthew • Matt 6:1

Prayer in Public

"And when you pray, don't act like phonies. They love to stand up and pray in houses of worship and on street corners, so they can show off in public. I swear to you, they have received all the reward they will ever get. "

Source: Matthew • Matt 6:5

Hidden remorse

When you fast, don't make a spectacle of your remorse as the pretenders do. As you know, they make their faces unrecognizable so they may be publicly recognized. I swear to you, they have been paid in full.

Source: Matthew • Matt 6:16

Love Your Enemies

But love your enemies, and do good, and lend, expecting nothing in return. *Your reward will be great,* and you'll be children of the most high.

Source: Q • Luke 6:35a

First Stone Gospel

Then everybody returned home, [1]but Jesus went to the Mount of Olives. [2]Early in the morning he showed up again in the temple area and everybody gathered around him. He sat down and began to teach them.

[3]The scholars and Pharisees bring him a woman who was caught committing adultery. They make her stand there in front of everybody, [4]and they address him, "Teacher, this woman was caught in the act of adultery. [5]In the Law Moses commanded us to stone women like this. What do you say?" ([6]They said this to trap him, so they would have something to accuse him of.)

Jesus stooped down and began drawing on the ground with his finger.

[7]When they insisted on an answer, he stood up and replied, "Whoever is sinless in this crowd should go ahead and throw the first stone at her." [8]Once again he squatted down and continued writing on the ground.

[9]His audience began to drift away, one by one – the elders were the first

to go – until Jesus was the only one left, with the woman there in front of him.

[10]Jesus stood up and said to her, "Woman, where is everybody? Hasn't
any one condemned you?"

[11]She replied, "No one, sir."

"I don't condemn you either," Jesus said. "You're free to go, but from now on no more sinning."

Source: First Stone Gospel • John 7:53–8:11

Rewards Are Intrinsic

In the everyday world people expect reward for good behavior and punishment for bad. Rewards and punishment play a fairly prominent role in the gospels, especially in Matthew, and elsewhere in the New Testament. The theme is particularly prominent in the Book of Revelation. Yet two very different views of these sanctions lie side-by-side in the gospels. They stand in strong contrast to each other. Both cannot represent the same wise mind. Which one stems from the historical Jesus?

On the one hand, Matthew has Jesus say, "Don't fear those who kill the body but cannot kill the soul; instead, you ought to fear the one who can destroy both the soul and the body in Gehenna."[1] This pronouncement appears to reflect a time when Christians are being persecuted and some face the prospect of martyrdom. Those under threat are being admonished to fear God more than the authorities, who have power only over the body, while God can assign both body and soul to Gehenna (the place where the wicked are punished after their death; hell is often a synonym for Gehenna). In the middle of the second century, a homily composed by an unknown author gave this additional explanation:

> Jesus said to Peter, "After their death the lambs should have no fear of the wolves. And you shouldn't be afraid of those who kill you and then can do nothing more to you. Save your fear for the one who can throw both body and soul into the fires of Gehenna after your death."[2]

This is how it will be at the end of the age:

1. Matt 10:28   2. 2 Clem 5:4

God's messengers will go out and separate the evil from the righteous and throw the evil into the fiery furnace. People in that place will weep and grind their teeth.[3]

All of this is confirmed by the so-called parable of the last judgment.[4] The account of the sheep and goats at the last judgment is not a parable and it did not originate with Jesus. In it, the goats receive this fate:

You, condemned to the everlasting fire prepared for the devil and his messengers, get away from me![5]

At the conclusion of the story, this summary:

The second group will then head for everlasting punishment, but the virtuous for everlasting life.[6]

A similar theme is expressed in the appendix to the parable of the wedding celebration in Matthew, an addition that depicts the fate of the guest who arrived without a wedding garment.[7] This notion of punishment appears to have been the special contribution of Matthew to the gospel tradition, although it appears less prominently in both Luke and Mark.

In contrast, Jesus teaches that rewards and punishment are intrinsic to the acts and thoughts to which they are related. Unlike John the Baptist, Jesus did not call to repentance and consequently did not threaten with the wrath of God. He does not make accusations of an ultimate nature, and he is not judgmental. Although he can be caustically critical, he does not condemn. His basic principle is reciprocity: "Forgive and you'll be forgiven" is his admonition.[8] He advises his followers to beg God to forgive their obligations to the same extent they have forgiven the debts owed to them.[9] His counsel is that God is generous to all alike; God causes the sun to shine on both the good and the bad, and he sends the rain on both the just and the unjust.[10] In other

3. Matt 13:49–50

4. Matt 25:31–46

5. Matt 25:41

6. Matt 25:46

7. Matt 22:11–13

8. Luke 6:37

9. Matt 6:12

10. Matt 5:45

words, God appears to be impartial. Jesus does not speak explicitly about the fate of persons after death.

When he does speak about reward, he does so in an ethical context:

> If you love those who love you,
> why should you be commended for that?
> Even the toll collectors do as much, don't they?[11]

> To sum up, you are to be as liberal in your love as your heavenly father is.[12]

The evangelist is aware of this line of Jesus' teaching. He gives expression to it in the framework he provides for complexes of sayings in the Sermon on the Mount. These formulations belong to Matthew or the tradition before him, but they do express the sentiment of Jesus:

> Take care that you don't flaunt your religion in public to be noticed by others. Otherwise, you will have no recognition from your Father in the heavens.[13]

> And when you pray, don't act like phonies. They love to stand up and pray in houses of worship and on street corners, so they can show off in public. I swear to you, they have received all the reward they will ever get.[14]

> When you fast, don't make a spectacle of your remorse as the pretenders do. As you know, they make their faces unrecognizable so their fasting may be publicly recognized. I swear to you, they have been paid in full.[15]

In sum, the rewards that Jesus offers are intrinsic to the deeds for which they are the reward, and the punishment consists in the lack of recognition that one is a child of God.

We can observe the two views of reward and punishment lying side-by-side in a passage in the sermon on the plain, which is

11. Matt 5:46
12. Matt 5:48
13. Matt 6:1

14. Matt 6:5
15. Matt 6:16

Luke's version of the Sermon on the Mount. After summarizing the preceding complex of sayings he has taken from the Sayings Gospel Q, Luke goes on to draw conclusions:

> But love your enemies,
> and do good, and lend,
> expecting nothing in return.
> *Your reward will be great,*
> and you'll be children of the Most High.[16]

Jesus has just spoken about loving enemies, doing good to those who have not treated you well, and lending money with no expectation of return. Then Luke adds, in apparent contradiction to the maxims Jesus has just formulated, "Your reward will be great." Line four amends line three. Line four has no parallel in Matthew, which means that it is Luke's invention; had it appeared in the Q text which both he and Matthew are copying and revising, Matthew almost certainly would have included it. This correction of the underlying Jesus tradition reveals how readily the evangelists permitted themselves to amend Jesus' vision with proverbial lore drawn from the received world.

Fictions and additions to the Jesus tradition are not always at odds with the historical figure. There are some "true fictions" – inventions true to the profile of Jesus as measured by other things he probably said or did. For example, the tale of the woman who was accused of adultery, found in some manuscripts of the Gospel of John and Luke, although a fiction, is a story that accurately reflects the disposition of Jesus.[17] The woman is brought to Jesus and he is asked whether she should be stoned in accordance with the law of Moses – where it is stipulated that a witness to a crime must throw the first stone.[18] Jesus responds with the suggestion that the person in the crowd who is without fault should cast the first stone. Only those without fault have the right to condemn and punish. All others should be grateful for mercy.

---

16. Luke 6:35
17. John 8:53–9:11

18. Deut 22:22–30; cf. 17:7

Humor
& Humility

13

Coat & Shirt

If someone sues you for your coat, give him the shirt off your back to go with it.

Source: Q • Matt 5:40

Award to the Poor

Congratulations, you poor!
God's domain belongs to you.

Source: Q • Luke 6:20

Give to Beggars

Give to everyone who begs from you.

Source: Q • Matt 5:42a

Lend without Return

If you have money, don't lend it at interest. Rather, give it to someone from whom you won't get it back.

Sources: Thomas, Q • Thom 95:1–2

Lost Coin

Is there any woman with ten silver coins, who if she loses one, wouldn't light a lamp and sweep the house and search carefully until she finds it? ⁹When she finds it, she invites her friends and neighbors over and says, "Celebrate with me, because I have found the silver coin I had lost."

Source: Luke • Luke 15:8–9

Lost Sheep

Is there any one of you who owns a hundred sheep and has one stray off, who wouldn't leave the ninety-nine in the wilderness, and go after the one that got lost until he finds it? ⁵And when he finds it, he lifts it up on his shoulders, happy. ⁶Once he gets home, he invites his friends and his neighbors over, and says to them, "Celebrate with me, because I have found my lost sheep."

Sources: Q, Thom • Luke 15:4–6

Unforgiving Slave

This is why Heaven's imperial rule should be compared to a secular ruler who decided to settle accounts with his slaves. ²⁴When the process began, this debtor was brought to him who owed ten million dollars. ²⁵Since he couldn't pay it back, the ruler ordered him sold, along with his wife and children and everything he had, so he could recover his money.

²⁶At this prospect, the slave fell down and groveled before him: "Be patient with me, and I'll repay every cent." ²⁷Because he was compassionate, the master of that slave let him go and canceled the debt.

²⁸As soon as he got out, that same fellow collared one of his fellow slaves who owed him a hundred dollars, and grabbed him by the neck and demanded: "Pay back what you owe!"

²⁹His fellow slave fell down and begged him: "Be patient with me and I'll pay you back."

³⁰But he wasn't interested; instead, he went out and threw him in prison until he paid the debt.

³¹When his fellow slaves realized what had happened, they were terribly distressed and went and reported to their master everything that had taken place.

³²At that point, his master summoned him: "You wicked slave," he says to him, "I canceled your entire debt because you begged me. ³³Wasn't it only fair for you to treat your fellow slave with the same consideration as I treated you?" ³⁴And the master was so angry he handed him over to those in charge of punishment until he paid back everything he owed.

Source: Matthew • Matt 18:23–34

Left & Right Hands

Don't let your left hand in on what your right hand is up to.

Sources: Matthew, Thomas • Matt 6:3

Sliver & Timber

You see the sliver in your friend's eye, but you don't see the timber in your own eye. ²When you take the timber out of your own eye, then you will see well enough to remove the sliver from your friend's eye.

Sources: Thomas, Q • Thom 26:1–2

Not What Goes In

It's not what goes into a person that can defile; It's what comes out that defiles.

Sources: Mark, Thomas • Mark 7:15

Emperor & God

Pay the emperor what belongs to the emperor and God what belongs to God.

Sources: Mark, Thomas • Mark 12:17b

Scholars' Privileges

Be on guard against the scholars who like to parade around in long robes, and who love to be addressed properly in the marketplaces, and who prefer important seats in the synagogues and the best couches at banquets.

Sources: Q, Mark • Luke 20:46

Pharisee & Toll Collector

Two men went up to the temple to pray, one a Pharisee and the other a toll collector.

[11]The Pharisee stood up and prayed silently as follows: "I thank you, God, that I'm not like everybody else, thieving, unjust, adulterous, and especially not like that toll collector over there. [12]I fast twice a week, I give tithes of everything that I acquire."

[13]Now the toll collector stood off by himself and didn't even dare to look up, but struck his chest, and muttered, "God, have mercy on me, sinner that I am."

[14]Let me tell you, the second man went back home acquitted, but the first one did not. For those who promote themselves will be demoted, but those who demote themselves will be promoted.

Source: Luke • Luke 18:10–14a

Saving One's Life

Whoever tries to hang on to life will forfeit it, but whoever forfeits life will preserve it.

Sources: Q, Mark, John • Luke 17:33

Humor
& Humility

Humor

Jesus' parables and aphorisms are laced with humor in the form of parody, paradox, hyperbole, ambiguity, and irony.

His saying about giving up one's shirt to go with a coat claimed under the law would have been a howler in a two-garment society. The consequences dawn belatedly on the listener – which is what makes it funny.

Extending congratulations to the poor for their most favored status must have brought smiles to many faces.

The global injunction to give to every beggar who asks stretches normal credulity.

The recovery of the lost coin pokes fun at the woman who is so grateful for her good luck that she then spends her coin to sponsor a celebration with friends.

The parable of the lost sheep is hilarious. It is a knee-slapper among peasants, who instantly understand that the recovered stray would be the victim of their celebration.

Then there is the slave who cannot understand the magnitude of generosity when forgiven a debt of ten million dollars. That generosity is contrasted with his own niggardliness in refusing to forgive an obligation of one hundred dollars. The contrast is grotesque.

Jesus' metaphors are rich in paradox. Try hiding what your right hand is doing from your left hand and you'll see how frustrating the exercise is – and how paradoxical. And the contrast between a sliver embedded in the eye and a timber sticking out of it is hyperbole at its most hyperbolic.

To these examples of humor running through the aphorisms and parables of Jesus, I might add one further instance. I believe the Markan version of the saying about what goes in is the original form:

It's not what goes into a person that can defile;
It's what comes out that defiles.[1]

This enigmatic saying was understood in the Jesus tradition as a saying about eating unclean foods. Unclean foods, Jesus says, do not defile, in spite of what you have been taught. To say that he didn't need more than the first line: "What goes into you can't defile you." "Eat whatever is set before you" would likewise suffice; it is among the instructions given to disciples when he sends them out on a preaching mission.[2] But he doesn't let it rest at that. He adds, "what comes out of you can defile you." Why does he make that addition?

What goes in, he says, cannot defile, but what comes out can and does. He doesn't specify which orifice in the human body he has in mind. We know that the first has to refer to the mouth, since that is the primary opening through which things are taken in. He thus declares that no foods are unclean. On the other hand, it is the lower orifice in a society without plumbing that is the source of most pollution. By contrasting the upper with the lower orifice, Jesus may have been indulging in a bit of humor to make an important point.

Those who transmitted this saying were not satisfied to leave the orifices unspecified, however. Matthew found the contrast easier to handle as a double reference to the mouth: "What goes into your mouth doesn't defile you; what comes out of your mouth does."[3] What comes out of your mouth presumably comes from the heart: sexual immorality, thefts, murders, adulteries, envies, wickedness, deceit, promiscuity, and evil eye, blasphemy, arrogance, lack of good sense. Very few of these things have to do specifically with the mouth. This list is incongruent with the contrast in the original saying. It is an example of overlooking the pungency of the aphorism in favor of an extended catalogue of virtues, or in this case, sins. In addition, the moralizing conclusion has now lost sight of the original point: there are no foods that defile.

1. Mark 7:15   2. Luke 10:8   3. Matt 15:11

Humor in most of its forms is inimical to moralism. Moralisms are the enemy of humor. Morality may be defined as conformity to established, sanctioned codes of behavior, as the acceptance of conventional notions of right and wrong. We have observed that Jesus was a social deviant. He was not a conformist; he was an iconoclast. He was therefore not a moralist. Indeed, we are obliged to acknowledge that it is not possible to derive rules of behavior directly from his parables and witticisms. What one can derive from them are guidelines, direction pointers, and paradigms that are useful in constructing an ethic.

Ambiguity is a tool Jesus employs to shift the responsibility for decision and action to his listeners, and thus avoid prescribing behavior for his followers. When he is asked whether one should pay taxes, he shifts the burden of decision on to the questioner with an equivocal response: pay the emperor what is due the emperor and pay God what is due God. In addition to refusing to be moralistic and prescriptive, he utilizes the power of humor in framing his responses so the inquirer can't escape the obvious conclusion.

Humility

Humor and humility are twins. Humor is the antidote for arrogance and hubris. It is very difficult to take ourselves and our pronouncements too seriously, if what we say and do is permeated with humor.

Humility is also the enemy of ostentation. Jesus pokes fun at pomposity in a variety of ways. He caricatures the learned scribes, who like to parade around in long robes. They insist on the proper address of respect in public places. They prefer important seats in synagogues and like the best couches at symposia, the banquets for the exchange of sophisticated conversation.

One of Jesus' most scathing attacks on ostentation is his parable contrasting a member of the purity party, that is, a pharisee, with a toll collector. The one boasts of his status before God, citing a list of the things he avoids and the tithes he does not avoid.

The toll collector, in contrast, begs for mercy as a sinner. He is unable to cite any achievements in his plea for mercy.

Humility gives birth to selflessness. Jesus apparently taught his disciples to be careless about life. In a saying preserved by Luke, Jesus warns that

> Whoever tries to hang on to life will forfeit it,
> but whoever forfeits life will preserve it.[4]

That is the ultimate paradox: lose life in order to gain life. It is perhaps the foundation of Jesus' ethic. It is certainly at the base of his trust ethic. It seems to mark his own disposition to life, a disposition that came to be symbolized in the cross.

The version of the saying cited above is probably derived from the Sayings Gospel Q. However, along the way some scribe added the qualifying phrase "for my sake." The saying is now on the way to being suitable for a martyrdom context. Mark expands the qualifier to include the gospel: "Remember, by trying to save your own life, you're going to lose it, but by losing your life for the sake of the gospel, you're going to save it."[5] That revision reflects the beginning of persecution of members of the Jesus movement.

The Fourth Gospel, on the other hand, remembers a purer form:

> Those who love life lose it,
> but those who hate life in this world will preserve it for
> unending, real life.[6]

Unfortunately, the Fourth Evangelist has put a negative stamp on life in the present world in favor of a positive reading of life in another, future realm. Those valuations are foreign to Jesus.

4. Luke 17:33
5. Mark 8:35

6. John 12:25

The End of Brokered Religion

14.

The Temple Incident

They come to Jerusalem. And he went into the temple and began chasing the vendors and shoppers out of the temple area, and he turned the bankers' tables upside down, along with the chairs of the pigeon merchants, [16]and he wouldn't even let anyone carry a container through the temple area. [17]Then he started teaching and would say to them: "Don't the scriptures say, 'My house is to be regarded as a house of prayer for all peoples'? – but you have turned it into 'a hideout for crooks'!"

Source: Mark • Mark 11:15–17

The Samaritan

This fellow was on his way from Jerusalem down to Jericho when he fell into the hands of robbers. They stripped him, beat him up, and went off, leaving him half dead. [31]Now by coincidence a priest was going down that road; when he caught sight of him, he went out of his way to avoid him. [32]In the same way, when a Levite came to the place, he took one look at him and crossed the road to avoid him. [33]But this Samaritan who was traveling that way came to where he was and was moved to pity at the sight of him. [34]He went up to him and bandaged his wounds, pouring olive oil and wine on them. He hoisted him onto his own animal, brought him to an inn, and looked after him. [35]The next day he took out two silver coins, which he gave to the innkeeper, and said, "Look after him, and on my way back I'll reimburse you for any extra expense you have had."

Source: Luke • Luke 10:30–35

Terms of Forgiveness (1)

Forgive and you'll be forgiven.

Source: Q • Luke 6:37c

Terms of Forgiveness (2)

Forgive our debts to the extent we have forgiven those in debt to us.

Source: Q • Matt 6:12

125

Lords of the Sabbath

The sabbath day was created for Adam and Eve, not Adam and Eve for the sabbath day. [28]So, the descendants of Adam lord it over the sabbath day.

Source: Mark • Mark 2:27–28

Rules for the Road (1)

When you go into any region, and walk about in the countryside, when people take you in, eat what they serve you.

Sources: Thomas, Q • Thom 14:4a

Rules for the Road (2)

Stay at that one house, eating and drinking whatever they provide.

Source: Q • Luke 10:7a

Scholars' Privileges

Within earshot of the people Jesus said to the disciples, [46]"Be on guard against the scholars who like to parade around in long robes, and who love to be addressed properly in the marketplaces, and who prefer important seats in the synagogues and the best couches at banquets. [47]They are the ones who prey on widows and their families, and recite long prayers just to put on airs. These people will get a stiff sentence!"

Sources: Mark, Q • Luke 20:45–47

Prayer in Private

When you pray, go into a room by yourself and shut the door behind you.

Source: Matthew • Matt 6:6

The End of Brokered Religion

The beginning of the Christian myth that became the foundation of the Christian religion is recorded by Paul of Tarsus:

I passed on to you as of paramount importance what I also had received: that Christ died for our sins according to the scriptures and that he was buried, and that he was raised "on the third day" according to the scriptures.[1]

Sometime during the course of the second century, in all probability, that myth was developed as the "Apostles' Creed," which then became standardized in the eighth century. The second article reads:

I believe in Jesus Christ, God's only Son, our Lord,
who was conceived by the Holy Spirit,
born of the Virgin Mary,
suffered under Pontius Pilate,
was crucified, died, and was buried;
he descended to the dead.
On the third day he rose again;
he ascended into heaven,
and he will come again to judge the living and the dead.

The historical figure of Jesus has been displaced in this version, except for the two lines that refer to his suffering, Pilate, his death and burial. It is essentially a creed with an empty center.

Yet the development was not yet complete. In the fourth century and beyond, the myth was expanded to include creation. According to Genesis, God created the heavens and the earth, man and women, and saw that the creation and creatures were

1. 1 Cor 15:3–4.

good. However, Adam and Eve, our primal progenitors, disobeyed God, were banished from paradise upon acquiring the knowledge of good and evil. With that knowledge came the sense of shame and guilt. And mortality. Universal mortality was the consequence of universal sin.

Augustine provided the theological frame of reference for this aspect of the myth. Adam and Eve's fall from grace was basically a fall into sexuality. The sin of Adam was passed on from generation to generation via the male sperm, which carried the virus. Unfortunately, God had not made provision for procreation without sex, so human beings were destined to go on sinning as they produced progeny.

The church, meanwhile, had worked this part of the story into the myth of the Christ. The sacrifice of Jesus Christ became the means to overcome human separation from the Holy God by virtue of Jesus' purity. After all, he was born of a virgin, who conceived him without sexual intercourse, so he was not tainted with the virus of Adam. And even his mother was delivered by divine decree from that taint in order to preserve her son's efficacy. As the perfect sacrifice, he was able to satisfy the requirements of a demanding God and so delivered human kind – at least those who "believe on him" – from Adam's mistake.

On the basis of this myth, the church went into business wholesale as a franchised salvation syndicate. Baptism became the water rite through which the condemned had to pass in order to have their sins washed away. (In later churches, the baptismal font was located outside the narthex so the sinners could pass through the waters on their way to the altar without defiling the sanctuary.) The eucharist was interpreted as a repetition of the blood sacrifice of Jesus, a repetition that took place with every mass. Sin was confessed with regularity during the liturgy and absolution was granted to the truly repentant.

Of course, the righteous died anyway – their mortality was intact, in spite of the fate of Jesus, their mentor. As an exception, Jesus was raised on the third day and ascended to the right hand of God. That, the pious hope, will be their destiny at the general resurrection.

In *Meeting Jesus Again for the First Time,* Marc Borg wrote that the notion that God's only son came to this planet to offer his life as a sacrifice for the sins of the world is simply incredible.[2] The interpretation of Jesus as both high priest and sacrificial victim (Epistle to the Hebrews) or as scapegoat was meant to displace the religion of the second temple, but instead it became the vehicle for retaining and maintaining religion brokered by a priest – only under new auspices. While the once-for-all sacrifice of Jesus was initially subversive of the priestly cult with its sacrificial system, it subsequently became the successor to that system. How difficult that myth is to swallow is indicated by the confession of Bishop Spong: "I would choose to loathe rather than to worship a deity who required the sacrifice of his son."[3]

Temple religion is a brokerage system in which priestly mediators are the necessary link between patrons like God and the emperor and those who seek favors. For Jesus, individuals have immediate, direct access to God. God's domain has no brokers. Jesus eliminates all brokers. That may be the reason he provoked the incident in the temple.[4] One interpretation of that event is that he objected to the commercialization of the temple cult. It may also be the reason he speaks disparagingly of priests and Levites in the parable of the Samaritan.[5] It may account for his scorn for scholars and their privileges.[6]

Jesus does not regard himself as a broker, at least as the synoptic gospels represent him. When the four let the paralytic down through the roof, Jesus notices their trust and says to the paralytic, "Child, your sins are forgiven!"[7] To the woman with a vaginal hemorrhage, Jesus says, "Daughter, your trust has cured you."[8] The conclusion to the story of blind Bartimaeus has Jesus saying to the patient, "Be on your way, your trust has cured you."[9] Jesus remarks the trust of the centurion, who pleads for his servant.[10] Matthew narrates the cure of two blind men, to whom Jesus

---

2. *Meeting Jesus Again,* p. 131.
3. *Why Christianity Must Change or Die,* p. 95.
4. Mark 11:15–17//Matt 21:12–13// Luke 19:45–46//John 2:13–17
5. Luke 10:30–35

6. Luke 20:46/Mark 12:38–39
7. Mark 2:5//Matt 9:2//Luke 5:20
8. Mark 5:34//Matt 9:22//Luke 8:48
9. Mark 10:52//Luke 18:43 (Matthew omits)
10. Matt 8:10

remarks, "Your trust will be the measure of your cure."[11] Jesus makes a similar remark to the Canaanite woman whose daughter he is about to cure.[12] To the woman who anoints Jesus' feet, Jesus says, "Your sins have been forgiven. . . . Your trust has saved you; go in peace."[13] Luke tells the story of the ten lepers. When one returns to express his gratitude, Jesus remarks, "Get up and be on your way; your trust has cured you."[14] Put pointedly, Jesus never tells those he has cured, "I have cured you." He never even says, "God has cured you." Access to divine healing requires no brokers.

Individuals are invited to function as their own brokers in relation to God. Those who require forgiveness can be forgiven only if they sponsor forgiveness: "*Forgive and you'll be forgiven,*" Jesus says.[15] Jesus is out of the loop; even God is out of the loop. In prayer, Jesus teaches his disciples to ask for the remission of debt only to the extent that they themselves have remitted the debts of others.[16] Petitioners are their own brokers.

Jesus recommends that the rich young man sell all he has and give the proceeds to the poor. He doesn't say give it to me, or give it to the temple.[17] The temple does not appear to be an intermediary linking the worshipper with God.

For Jesus, God's domain is also apparently a domain without cult rituals. The ancient sacrificial system was erected on the notion that the gods required some sacrifice, some gift, to appease them. But the idea of atonement certainly does not stem from Jesus. Indeed, it contravenes his fundamental dedication to a brokerless kingdom.

The same can be said of baptism. The practice is probably a carryover from earlier allegiances to John the Baptist. Jesus' indifference to purity codes and his apparent lack of interest in repentance suggest that the Fourth Gospel is correct: Jesus did not baptize; the practice belonged to his disciples, probably those who had previously been followers of John.[18]

11. Matt 9:29
12. Matt 15:28
13. Luke 7:50
14. Luke 17:19

15. Luke 6:37
16. Matt 6:12
17. Mark 10:17–22
18. John 4:2

And sabbath regulations and purity codes appear not to apply in God's domain. To human status and needs Jesus subordinates sabbath requirements:

> The sabbath day was created for Adam and Eve,
> not Adam and Eve for the sabbath day.
> So, the descendants of Adam lord it even over the sabbath day.[19]

When he dispatches disciples on a preaching mission, he advises them to eat whatever their hosts provide along the way. That is certainly an accommodating approach to whatever Jewish food restrictions were in place in Galilee in his day. It suggests that Jesus had a generally permissive attitude towards traditional customs and codes.

Jesus' attitudes toward fasting and public piety are congruent with his notion of a brokerless, cultless, and codeless kingdom: fasting is not compatible with celebration, and those who practice public piety have received all the reward they will ever get, as is suggested by his counsel to pray in a closet with a closed door.[20]

A brokered religion produces a cyclical understanding of the faithful life: sin, guilt, forgiveness – the latter at the hands of the church and priest, of course. In addition, it tends to produce a passive relation to the Christian life, as Marc Borg also reminds us.[21] Since Christ has already died for our sins, it is not necessary that we should undergo a spiritual transformation. That passivity is carried over into the social, economic, and political realms as well: we are inclined to accept the world as it is rather than attempt to transform it. Furthermore, Borg goes on, brokered religion is oriented to the afterlife rather than to this life. We believe now in order to enjoy salvation later. For those without an innate sense of guilt about their origin, this form of Christianity is simply incredible.

19. Mark 2:27–28
20. Matt 6:6

21. *Meeting Jesus Again*, p. 130–32.

The Unkingdom of the UnGod

15.

The myth of God as king comes to powerful expression in Psalm 144:[1]

I will laud you, O God, my King,
I will extol your name for all ages to come.

. . . .

All your creatures will testify to you, O Lord,
All the faithful will extol you.
They will herald the glory of your kingdom
And speak of your majesty
in order to reveal your majesty to all human beings,
 along with the glorious grandeur of your kingdom.
Your kingdom is an everlasting kingdom,
and your dominion extends to every generation.[2]

In attempting to depict the exalted position of God, the ancients could do no better than compare God to the oriental monarch, whose power was absolute and whose opulence was as great as resources could provide. The song of Moses, recorded in Exodus 15, rehearses the mighty deeds of Yahweh and then bursts out in exaltation at the conclusion: "The Lord will reign forever and ever and ever."[3]

The myth of God as king is one of the symbolic paradigms by which Israel interpreted its history. The dominion

---

1. The translation is of the Greek text; in Hebrew and most English versions it is Psalm 145.

2. Psalm 144:1, 10–13
3. Exod 15:18

of her God extends to the remote past, to the creation in fact, and will endure for all ages to come. In addition, of course, Yahweh reigns over the present, with both positive and negative consequences. Yahweh raises up the fallen and protects those who observe the covenants, yet Yahweh also punishes — especially the enemies of Israel, but also God's own people when they stray from prescribed ways.

In the storied history of Israel, the period when God's kingdom was most perfectly embodied on earth was during the reigns of David and Solomon. During the time of David, the boundaries of Israel were presumably extended to their maximum, and, according to the legend, Solomon was the supreme builder of temples and national monuments. That idealized past became the content of the myth of God's reign when Israelites spoke of it in later generations.

Scholars have generally agreed that the parables and aphorisms of Jesus refer to something called the realm of God or God's domain. In view of the history of that symbolic representation of God, his reference may well be ironic. In any case, there is an anomaly in the juxtaposition of the *kingdom* of God and the vision of Jesus.

The authentic parables and aphorisms do not make use of the royal epic of Israel in their subject matter. The kingdom of the parables is not the kingdom of David and Solomon. On the contrary, the sayings of Jesus demote the royal line, assign the powerful and wealthy to an inferior position, and promote the poor, the tearful, and the dispossessed to the status of a privileged class. It is a kingdom of nobodies.

Jesus' listeners were not prepared for the irony. Jesus does not alert them to his design. The parables and aphorisms simply undermine the conceptual network associated with the Davidic kingdom and its apocalyptic successor, as depicted, for example, in the book of Revelation. Nevertheless, for Jesus God is sovereign; Jesus advocates complete trust in God the Father. Yet God does not behave like an oriental monarch. God is not a cosmic bully; God does not force humans to act as they are instructed.

God's majesty, as Jesus sees it, is reduced by comparison to the pride, avarice, and opulence of Near Eastern monarchs. Jesus elects the underside of the social world as the heroic. Outsiders become insiders, as it were, and insiders are left out. The plots of the parables and the themes of the aphorisms subvert the expected meaning of the primary referent, the kingdom of God. For Jesus, the realm of God is the unkingdom of the unGod.

To be an "insider" in the kingdom one must be an "outsider." That requirement is never rescinded. A sinner is an "outsider" – from the standpoint of those who thought they were insiders. In God's domain, Christians may be insiders but they are without privilege. Christians or insiders are never superior to non-Christians (outsiders). Christians are not the exclusive brokers of God's grace. The irony is that many Christians claim superiority and monopoly in the name of the Jesus who never claimed anything for himself – and who insisted that his disciples ask nothing for themselves.

The Domain of God as Mythic Destination

16.

The movement of Jesus from habituated convictions to new ways of viewing the world and the humans who people it suggests another way of formulating Jesus' overall vision of God's domain. Jesus was taking leave of some restrictive aspects of his ancestral patterns of behavior and was setting out for a promised land of new kinship and behavior codes.

The movement away from and towards is reminiscent of the myth of the exodus. The Israelites set out from Egypt for a land on the other side of the wilderness only to wander for forty years in the desert, with nothing to sustain them except daily manna from heaven and water struck from a rock. (Those two features make their journey both mythic and epic at the same time.) And in a sense they never quite got to the promised land. (Someone has wryly observed that the Israelites might have gotten to the Jordan much sooner had Moses been willing to stop and ask for directions.) Moses was not permitted to cross the water, although he could see his destination from afar. (Mythic destinations can be viewed only from afar.) Those who did cross the Jordan found themselves entangled in the culture of the Canaanites and so were very little better off than they had been in Egypt. Indeed, the archaeological evidence now seems to demonstrate that those who came to possess the new land had been there all along; they were not refugees from an alien space, but indigenous peoples who were struggling for a new identity.

The moral of this epic tale seems to be that the promised land is some hypothetical destination which we are not permitted to reach. There will always be some further desert to cross, some new challenge to meet, some new enemy to love, some new attachments to forsake, some new boundaries to cross. It is the journey and not the arrival that constitutes our salvation. This is the ultimate vision of Jesus.

As Christian orthodoxy developed, it adopted not the exodus or even the exile as its primary paradigm, but the myth of the external redeemer. Jesus is assigned the title role. In that myth, the redeemer drops down out of heaven into human space, performs some miracles to certify his legitimacy, dies on the cross as the final sacrifice, and returns to heaven. His first coming will be followed by his second coming, when he returns to finish what he did not do on the first trip. That hero does for us what we cannot do for ourselves. That redeemer figure is greater than David, greater than Solomon, indeed, more powerful than Caesar.

The myth of the Exodus assumes an internal redeemer who is flawed from the outset. Moses cannot achieve; he can only point. He catches sight of his goal, but dies just as he is about to cross over. The orthodox Christian myth, on the other hand, imagines a mythic destination that is otherworldly and thus fundamentally different from the terminus of either the Exodus or the Exile. It borrows aspects from the old myth of God as king but transfers the locus of God's rule to another reality, to a heavenly realm. The Israelites thought they were coming home; Christians came to believe their real home was elsewhere, that they were perpetual aliens in a hostile environment. That has distorted their relationship to the planet in fundamental ways.

Jesus, on the other hand, seems to think that God's rule is present here and now albeit unseen, invisible. The hand of God is not apparent in the affairs of human beings and only obliquely in the ways of nature. Yet Jesus acts as though God's peculiar way of dealing with creation is the ultimate reality. Given that conviction, he can act only in accordance with its premises. So he trusts his vision, triggers celebrations, and creates communities out of the rabble he encounters along the road. His road is never ending; it goes on forever and ever, just as God's rule is unending. God's domain is a mythic destination, like the promised land. We can have it only if we do not possess it. That is the ultimate irony of Jesus' talk about God's realm.

The Cross as Symbol of Integrity

17.

Symbols have lives of their own, quite apart from human will and intention. Root symbols live and die out of the deep needs of the human psyche. But root symbols are also nourished by the institutions that adopt and employ them. We can reform symbols but we cannot create them out of nothing and we cannot will their demise.

Historic symbols come to life under a converging set of circumstances that endow them with uncanny powers. Once given life, they attract and carry with them endless accretions of overtone and significance. The cross as the primary icon of the Christian faith is such a symbol.

The cross did not take on heavy symbolic ballast until the fourth century. Constantine's vision at Milvian Bridge in 312 C.E. was the turning point. His vision consisted of a long golden spear with a transverse bar attached to give it the proper form. And the inscription thereon read "In this Sign Conquer." The rest, as they say, is history. And so the cross became the emblem of Christian triumphalism, forged in the fires of the late Roman empire, in the process of a military victory.

The victory of Constantine led to the veneration of "the true cross," fragments of which suddenly appeared everywhere. Those tiny fragments, according to James Carroll, gave birth to the saying "knock on wood," a kind of talisman to ward off bad luck.[1] The discovery and veneration of fragments of the true cross, of the nails employed to affix

1. *The Cross of Constantine*, p. 199.

141

Jesus to the timbers, of the sign Pilate placed over Jesus' head, of the crown of thorns, the whip, and the seamless robe together sprang to life under sponsorship of Helena, Constantine's pious mother. Constantine added to the emerging legend by erecting monuments all over the empire in honor of his mother's devotion. Many sacred sites, unknown earlier, were identified in the fourth century. By the sixth they were marked with monumental buildings.

The Crusades were launched under the banner of the cross in 1096 and the ground was laid for "Onward Christian Soldiers." Thousands joined in the Crusades as soldiers with the cross emblazoned on their garments marched across Europe and then Asia slaughtering Jews, Muslims, and pagans alike, all in the name of the humble Galilean – or rather, under the sign of the cross, now empty of its Jewish body.

The Crusades were followed in due course by the Inquisition. Initiated in 1232 by Frederick II and Pope Gregory IX, it lasted for more than six hundred years down into the nineteenth century. Its high point was the expulsion of Jews and Muslims from Spain in 1492. Women as witches came under its purview as well, thousands of whom died at the stake as a result. All this, too, under the sign of the cross. Recently, the archives of the church related to the Inquisition were opened to inspection. One student of those files remarked that an explanation for the Holocaust lies buried in those records.

The cross at Auschwitz is perhaps the supreme example of the potency of the Christian symbol and the unintended perversion to which it can be subject. Hovering over the place where thousands of Jews and others were murdered, it is a grotesque anomaly. Even the term "Holocaust" no longer seems appropriate, since that word means "burnt offering:" The proper term is *Shoah*, which means "catastrophe" or "disaster." As James Carroll puts it, the term signifies the absence rather than the presence of God.[2]

I am not at all certain that the symbol of the cross can be redeemed, can be freed from its triumphalist associations and evil

---

2. *The Cross of Constantine*, p. 11.

overtones. The symbol has moved a long way from Paul of Tarsus' notion of the cross as a manifestation of God's weakness in the salvific process. According to Paul, some look for miracles and portents, others depend on human wisdom for truth; the message of the cross he proclaims contradicts both. The power of God lies precisely in God's weakness, in God's unwillingness to satisfy human demands and aspirations. The content of that message Paul believed to be symbolized in baptism, which he took to mean dying to the world, that is, to the norms of the world, just as Jesus had done.[3] He also believed that his message should not be confused with his rhetoric, lest the meekness of Christ be compromised by Paul's show of wisdom.[4] The glory of the Christ, he reasoned, was exhausted in the cross, for it meant that he had died to the world and the world had died to him. True faith was not to be measured by worldly standards, but by the standard of the cross. That contains echoes of Jesus' vision of the invisible kingdom and trust ethic, both of which fly in the face of convention and received wisdom.

In the Christian epic codified in the Apostles' Creed, the story of Jesus culminates in the cross, and the cross means that Christ died for our sins. The cross in that myth is indelibly linked to the understanding of Jesus' death as a sacrificial atonement. That link supports the church as a salvation machine which feeds on human guilt for its sustenance. And it is linked to the Christian claim that salvation is possible only under the sign of the cross. That claim is the legacy of Constantine and the feudal monarchy, now embodied in the Roman church. We can no longer tolerate either of these connotations of the cross. We must abandon and suppress them if the cross is to survive as symbol.

John Hick has summarized the implications of the symbol of the cross when it stands for the Christian myth taken literally. His words are worth quoting:

> When the Christian myth is taken literally its central theme develops dangerous implications. For if Jesus was literally God,

---

3. Perhaps best spelled out in Romans 6.   4. 1 Cor 1:17–18

in the sense of being the second Person of the Godhead living a human life, it follows that Christianity alone among the world religions was founded by God in person, and is thus God's own religion, uniquely superior to all others. This conviction was used to validate Europe's conquest of most of what today we call the Third World, carrying off many of its inhabitants as slaves, exploiting its economies and destroying its cultures. The idea that Jesus was God likewise validated the Christian persecution of the Jews, who were held guilty of deicide, thus creating a deep-seated prejudice within the European psyche which continued in the secular anti-Semitism of the nineteenth and twentieth centuries, culminating in the Holocaust of the 1940s. When taken literally, the Christian myth becomes a supremacist ideology which, in conjunction with human greed, pride and prejudice, has used the name of Christ to justify profoundly unchristlike acts.[5]

The proclamation of the first missionaries (the Greek term for it is kerygma) and the derivative creed may not be entirely appropriate for the gospel of Jesus. The kerygma and creed are preoccupied with the status of Jesus rather than with God's domain; with the king rather than the kingdom; with an icon rather than the iconoclast. The members of the early Jesus movement were preoccupied with the status of the apostles and themselves, rather than with Jesus' vision of a boundaryless, brokerless community. The evidence is that they created a creed with an empty center: There is very little left of the Jesus of the parables and aphorisms in that creed.

The Jesus of the parables and aphorisms becomes the victim of his own vision; he dies with his trust in God inviolate; he has learned to be indifferent to life in the bosom of that trust. He frames his admonitions for himself; he tells his parables as though he were hearing them. The cross, in retrospect, is the symbol of that integrity. As Socrates chose to drink the hemlock rather than deny the law its due, so in a similar way the cross

5. *The Fifth Dimension*, p. 237.

expresses Jesus' surrender to his vision. He was unwilling to compromise his vision for the sake of survival, for the sake of expediency, for the sake of success. Absolute, uncompromising integrity is the true meaning of the cross.

The coming radical transformation of the Christian tradition will attempt to recover that Jesus and translate his vision into terms suitable for the twenty-first century.

An Alternative Reality

The Narrow Door

Struggle to get in through the narrow door; I'm telling you,
many will try to get in, but won't be able.

Sources: Q, Thomas • Luke 13:24

od's domain is an alternative reality.
There is a door opening on to that reality, but the door is narrow and difficult
to find. Why is that so? First of all,
because God's domain is subversive of
the old order. One has to be predisposed
to let go of the old and comfortable in
order to embark on the quest for the new.
Only then does one have a chance to find the door. But the
old reality is tenacious. It has a powerful grip on us because
it is supported by the vast majority of human beings in our
own and other communities. Its gravitational pull is exceptionally strong. It has the power of a black hole. It tends to
swallow up all other alternatives.

In the second place, the door opens on to another world,
a world that is full of anomalies and dislocations in relation
to the default world. In it the old realities have been
rearranged and reconfigured in surprising ways. The result is
a counter reality, one that retains the ordinary features of
the old world but reconceived and rearticulated. The
prospect is bewildering and hence frightening to the faint-
hearted.

To put matters more prosaically, the world we human beings inhabit is socially constructed. If we want to change that world, we must collectively deconstruct the old world and then collectively fabricate its replacement. That is a formidable challenge. But these are the only conditions under which the imperial rule of God can arrive.

Of course, Jesus did not think in these abstract categories. His vision of "the coming" of God's imperial rule was concrete and specific. By scrutinizing his admonitions and pronouncements and by examining his parables, we can see how he imagined God's rule to be realized. How he addressed his listeners will betray how he expected God's imperial rule to "arrive."

The coming of God's domain: Admonitions & injunctions

How will God's domain come, according to Jesus? His preliminary answer was, "It will not come by looking for it, by saying, 'here it is' or 'there it is.'" It does not arrive on the wings of signs and portents, of miracles and divine interventions. On the contrary, the language of Jesus tells us that it comes via human action. The repertoire of his authentic sayings is filled with admonitions and injunctions addressed to human beings. About a third of his basic sayings fall into that category. (Table 1 contains a list of those admonitions.)

You are to love enemies, but hate families, he enjoins; that will enlarge the circle of humanity, on the one hand, but break the stranglehold of the patriarchal enclave, on the other. You are to undermine the system by turning the other cheek, by including the shirt off your back when sued for your cloak, and by going the second mile when conscripted. You are to settle on the way to court in order to avoid the inequities of the judicial system. You are to lend money to those from whom you can't collect interest, or better yet, from whom you can't expect to recover the principal. That goes together with the admonition to sell one's goods and give the proceeds to the poor.

These are all things human beings can do to effect the arrival of God's domain.

In God's domain, we are urged not to fret about life, about food and clothing. We are to be as confident in divine providence as are the flowers of the field and the birds of the air. We are to give to every beggar who approaches us, and not let our left hand know that our right hand has so acted. We are to forget obligations to dead parents and let the dead bury the dead.

Again, Jesus urges his followers to act in these specific ways as children of God.

In God's realm, we are to ask and expect to receive, seek and expect to find, knock in the certainty that a door will be opened. That confidence is expressed in the petition to provide us with bread for the day, a request literally addressed to God but in fact directed to other human beings. Jesus never suggests that manna will fall out of heaven or that some miracle will result in the multiplication of loaves and fish. God's largesse comes by way of the generosity of others. It is the rule in honor/shame societies that hospitality is expected, indeed required, when a request is advanced on behalf of a late traveler. The same can be said of debts – real money debts. One prayer petition asks that our debts be remitted to the extent we have remitted the debts of others. Once again, it is literally a prayer addressed to God, but its fulfillment depends on the actions of human beings who are under obligation to each other. God is not expected to interfere or to rectify an injustice or imbalance. Mortals are expected to achieve that goal for themselves.

Table 1. The Admonitions and injunctions of Jesus
love your enemies
hate your father and mother
turn the other cheek
give the shirt off your back
go a second mile
settle on the way to court
lend money without interest

sell your goods and give to the poor
give to every beggar
don't fret about life, food, clothing
don't let your left hand know what your right hand does
let the dead bury the dead
look at the birds
notice the lilies
ask, seek, knock, and expect a positive response
give us bread for the day
forgive us our debts to the extent we forgive others theirs
forgive in order to be forgiven
Take the timber out of your own eye
let the children come
be generous in love
pay the emperor and God their due
guard against scholars
on the road, eat what is set before you
on the road, stay in one house

Correspondingly, if we covet forgiveness for moral or personal offences, we are to forgive the offences of others directed at ourselves: the relationship between the two is reciprocal. In the same vein, we are to extract the timber so obviously sticking out of our own eye before we seek to remove the sliver in our neighbor's.

We are to grant children their place in God's order, along with women, toll collectors, prostitutes, lepers, and others at the margins of society. Jesus urges his followers to be as generous in their love as God is, who sends the rain on the just and unjust, and causes the sun to shine on both good and evil. God, it seems, is generous to the ungrateful and wicked.

Jesus admonishes his followers to pay the emperor whatever is due the emperor and to reserve the proper obligation for God, whatever that is. He urges them to guard against scholars who like pretense and pomp. When on the road, disciples are to eat what is set before them, purity regulations aside, and stay put in quarters offered them in hospitality rather than shop for better chambers.

All these are admonitions addressed to his listeners, disciples and others alike, in fulfillment of the conditions of God's rule. Jesus does not invoke God's intervention now or in the future in the fulfillment of these conditions. He does not indulge in oracular speech, as though he were receiving the message directly from God. He does not appeal to the temple, or the priests, or scripture to support his injunctions. He simply takes it for granted that these conditions are fundamental to a world directly under God's care.

The coming of God's rule: Pronouncements

There is a second major strand in Jesus' discourse. That strand consists of pronouncements or 'is' statements. If the first group consists of imperatives or 'do' statements, the second category in his repertoire seeks to establish the basic values or status of persons and things in God's domain. This kind of language is called performative language. Performative language accomplishes something by statement or pronouncement. When the judge sentences someone to a prison term or announces a verdict that one party owes another a money debt, he or she is using performative language. The pronouncement itself achieves its goal. When the jury says, 'Not guilty,' the prisoner's status is modified. When minister or priest declares that man and woman are husband and wife it is the creation of a new status for the two involved. A coroner's declaration that a person is dead changes the legal status of that person. Jesus employs performative language frequently, perhaps even more frequently than he utilizes imperatives. (His pronouncements are summarized in Table 2.)

Jesus rarely speaks directly about the status of God's domain. However, in one pronouncement he does so. In declaring that God's domain is present but invisible to the unaided eye, he suggests in effect that the problem is with sight rather than the reality of God's imperial rule. What makes God's domain difficult to see? It is difficult to see because it is the counter reality to the default world we inhabit as a matter of course. The default world is not the real world, according to Jesus; that world is powerfully present but fundamentally unreal. The really real is actually something like the opposite of the world as it is customarily perceived.

The fundamental problem for those who are deceived by the everyday mentality is that in God's domain things run the other way around: they are reversed. The first are last and the last first is Jesus' basic dictum. Those who want to be first must be last of all and servant of all. Those who try to hang on to life will end by losing life, but those who forfeit life will preserve life.

Table 2. The Pronouncements of Jesus

God's domain is present but invisible
the first are last, the last first
number one is last and servant of all
those who hang on to life will forfeit it
those who forfeit life will preserve it
God's domain belongs to you poor
you hungry will have a feast
you tearful will laugh
you are worth more than a flock of sparrows
you are worth more than the lilies
you are worth more than the grass
You cannot extend life by taking thought
God counts the hairs on your head
God sends rain on good and bad
God causes the sun to shine on just and unjust
Camels (wealthy) cannot get through the eye of a needle
It is difficult for wealthy to get into God's domain
no one can serve two masters
foxes have dens, but Jesus has nowhere to lay his head
prophets are without honor on their home turf
Able-bodied don't need a doctor; the sick do
Satan fell from heaven
If Satan is divided, his rule is over

Adam & Eve are lords of the sabbath
What goes in does not pollute; what comes out does
Those not against us are for us
One potter made both inside and outside of the cup
God's domain is peopled with children
God's domain is peopled with lepers
God's domain is peopled with toll collectors & prostitutes
True relatives are those who do God's will
Your heavenly Father is liberal in love
fasting is not appropriate at a wedding
The door to God's domain is narrow
You cannot add to longevity by fretting about it
young wine is not stored in old wineskins
aged wine is not stored in new wineskins
After drinking aged wine no one wants young wine
There is nothing hidden that won't be revealed
No one lights a lamp and places it under a basket
A city sitting on top of a hill cannot be concealed
You do not pick grapes from thorns or figs from thistles
Those who promote themselves will be demoted
Those who demote themselves will be promoted

These are antithetical couplets that constitute paradoxes. How can the last actually be first? How can a person be number one by becoming servant of all? How can forfeiting life actually produce life? Jesus appears to be asserting that in God's domain things are not what they seem; in fact, they are the opposite of what they seem.

A fundamental reversal for Jesus is the status of the poor versus the rich. The poor are congratulated as the proprietors of God's domain. The hungry and the bereaved will feast and laugh. God cares for the birds and flowers, but human beings are more precious than these life forms. God is deeply concerned with life: he even counts the hairs on human heads. Fundamentally, God provides food and clothing for one and all, just as God sends the rain and sun on all indiscriminately.

The rich, on the other hand, have difficulty squeezing through the narrow door to God's domain — about as much difficulty as a camel attempting to squeeze through the eye of a needle. The wealthy are like the rich farmer who prospered, built storehouses for his wealth, and then died unexpectedly. The bind for the rich is that they cannot serve two masters, according to a proverb Jesus quotes. The one master that does not produce the desired end is wealth.

We have noted that Jesus does not indulge in self-reference, as a rule. There are two or three possible exceptions. In one he may be comparing himself to foxes with their dens and birds with their nests, when he confesses that he has no roof over his head. If that is a personal reference, he is contrasting himself with the customary status of persons with permanent addresses. Another reference to self may be the proverb that stipulates prophets are not honored on their home turf. He does not ordinarily claim prophetic status for himself. A third may be another proverbial saying: "The able-bodied don't need a doctor; it's the sick who do." Whether he thought of himself as a physician is difficult to say, since his language here, as elsewhere, is highly figurative. The allusions to prophets and doctors, if self-referential, are drawing on typifications rather than contrasts: Everyone knows that prophets are not honored at home and doctors are for the sick.

The everyday world of Jesus was filled with demons. Demons haunted wet places, such as springs and outhouses, and took possession of the feeble-minded and mentally ill. As an inhabitant of that world, Jesus announces that he saw Satan plummet from heaven, probably to his demise. In any case, he agrees that if he has exorcised demons, then God's rule has arrived; this means that divine rule and Satanic rule are diametrically opposed. The figure of the powerful man defending his property against robbers represents Satan or Beelzebul, who has to be tied up before the house can be cleared of evil spirits. The accusation that Jesus himself may be demon-possessed or mad or in league with Satan is met with the proverbial claim that a household divided against itself cannot stand. If Jesus drives out demons in the name of

Satan, then Satan is on his way out. It is a rhetorical ploy to fend off a charge based on everyday experience of the world. God's domain, in contrast, is devoid of the demonic. In retrospect, this is one feature of Jesus' vision that now appears truly 'prophetic.'

In his 'do' statements, Jesus advocates infringing the purity codes by encouraging disciples to eat whatever is set before them. In his 'is' statements he again infringes religious codes by asserting that Adam & Eve – ciphers for human beings – are the lords of the sabbath; they are the intended regulators and beneficiaries of sabbath observance. He further announces that nothing that goes in can defile, only what comes out. Here again, he is apparently abrogating regulations regarding foods.

The reality of God's domain is inclusive in ways that the default world is not. In one sweeping generalization, Jesus proclaims that those not against us are for us. This aphorism is quoted in the context of non-Jesus people exorcising demons. That is a way to include all those who endorse a demonless world and who do not actively opt out. The reverse is also found in the Jesus tradition: those not for us are against us. The double form of this saying may suggest that it is impossible to remain neutral.

Inclusiveness is the rule in God's domain, whereas exclusiveness is the rule in communities with high social and ethnic boundaries. The cup to be washed has both an inside and an outside, and both are the work of the potter. One potter, one cup. There is no way to segregate inside and outside. The Jesus community has no inside and outside. It includes children, lepers, toll collectors, prostitutes, sinners, all of whom are outsiders in the default world. Their inclusion comports with the God who sends rain and sun on all indifferently. It is for that reason that Jesus insists that all who do the will of God are his true relatives. Their behavior is what makes them children of God. Pronouncements and admonitions are joined in the last analysis: behavior determines status in God's domain. But it is not a set of moralisms that defines proper behavior. The proper behavior is to exit the received world and enter the new reality, the domain of God.

The coming of God's rule: The Parables

Like the aphorisms, the parables are a door opening on to an alternative reality. The parables assign certain features to that alternative reality, features that are important to observe.

The parables are about present reality

The parables do not expect God to intervene at some future date and establish God's domain. The parables are not eschatological, except in some poetic sense. God's domain for Jesus was an enchantment, in which past and future flowed together in the intensity of the present moment. Poets are known to have been overwhelmed by the convergence of the ecstasies of time. In those moments, they do not distinguish past, present, and future. For Jesus, God's domain was immediately and powerfully present, as though he stood with God at creation and with God at the eschaton, and understood the full intermediate ebb and flow of history. When disenchantment set in, following his death, God's domain was pushed off into some future by his followers, first into the immediate future, and then into the distant future, because they had lost the overpowering presence of God. And if God's domain were to come in the future, there would be a delay, and a delay required a second coming of the messiah—of Jesus— to achieve what his first coming had not. In other words, the overwhelming vision of Jesus was translated back into ordinary apocalyptic expectations of that time, expectations that some of Jesus' followers had learned from John the Baptist. The vision of Jesus was thereby domesticated, assimilated to conventional apocalyptic views.

The parables are devoid of recipe knowledge

The parables do not provide practical advice for performing simple tasks; they are devoid of recipe knowledge. The knowledge most of us use everyday consists of formulas for performing routine tasks. We know how to feed and clothe ourselves, we know how to get to work and fulfill the obligations of a job, and we know how to make an appointment with the doctor when we get sick. Knowledge of this kind is called recipe or procedure knowledge. Jesus does not offer concrete advice in his parables and aphorisms, in spite of the fact that his narrative fictions are filled with everyday situations and events. He offers no recipes for achieving mundane goals. He does not tell his followers how to succeed as merchants or how to attain happiness. His disciples looked to him for advice they could use, but he steadily refused to accommodate them. Jesus was preoccupied with a knowledge that lay beyond the horizons of the everyday world. As a consequence, he refused to be explicit and so avoided endorsements. His attention was riveted on his Father's will, so to speak, that is, on the threshold of knowledge that constitutes a new horizon within which to live.

The parables lack closure

There is no closure for the parables; they are open-ended. They do not teach a lesson; they subvert the world humans adopt as their paramount reality. God's domain lies across the way, in some fabulous yonder. For that reason, we must conclude that Jesus was not a moralist – by which I mean, he did not formulate and endorse specific rules of behavior. What he did endorse is absolute trust in the Father, which entails complete trust in the neighbor, in the chance encounter along the road. To trust God absolutely is to become careless about life, indifferent to the claims and expectations of the natural self and the everyday world humans inhabit. To be anxious about life is to miss the door to God's domain.

The parables are not self-referential

In the Jesus Seminar, we discovered that the parables were not self-referential. Jesus was not talking about himself. He appears only in the penumbra of the story, in its shadow, as the narrator. God does not appear in the parables either; God stands in the umbra of the story, in the zone of darkness beyond the horizon of the narrative. There is no latent christology buried in them, other than the risk entailed by accepting the invitation to cross over to some strange land where things run the other way around, as in Alice's looking glass.

Jesus' vision has the priority. The reality of his vision is the world to which Jesus gives himself. He is responding to the lure, the call of that reality. He is what he is by virtue of that reality. (The relation between self and world is dialectical: we create our worlds and then our worlds create us.) For that reason, it can be said that Jesus tells his parables and makes his pronouncements as though they were being spoken *to* him.

The parables subvert God's domain

The parables are only ironically appropriate to Jesus' vision of God's domain. They do not feature empires and emperors; rather, they trade in the trivial; they feature commonplaces and the ordinary. They elect the underside of the social world as the heroic. The poor, the unclean, the prostitutes, the toll collectors—all who have been marginalized – become privileged in God's domain. The outsiders become insiders, as it were, and the insiders become outsiders. The plot of the parables thus subverts the expected meaning of its primary referent, God's domain. They are even less suited to the commonly anticipated apocalyptic restoration. The symbol of God's domain is an ironic symbol: it means something like the opposite of what it connotes.

The real epic of Israel, of course, is not the story of Saul, David, and Solomon, but the myth of the Exodus. The epic of the Davidic kingdom endorses traditional values: power, wealth, position, authority. The Exodus, on the other hand, is inaugurated by the departure of slaves from Egypt, followed by years of wandering in the Sinai desert. That epic is more appropriate to the parables. But as Christian orthodoxy developed, it adopted the myth of the external redeemer as its epic, as the story which functions as the narrative frame for Jesus of Nazareth. In the myth of the outside redeemer, the hero is supernatural: he or she performs acts beyond the ability of normal human beings. However, in God's domain, as Jesus depicts it, the lowest of the low have the power to do everything for themselves by putting their trust in the Father. To have forgiveness all they need do is forgive others. They need only ask and they will receive. The parables call for repeated departure from Egyptian slavery and wandering in the desert. The parables thus undermine their own primary referent, God's domain.

In the orthodox myth, on the other hand, the parable is transformed into a history of salvation. In the Prodigal, the father we are told stands for God; the older son represents an unrepentant Israel; but then the orthodox interpreter refuses to name the younger son as the model of the Christian. Krister Stendahl, the former dean of the Harvard Divinity School, has said that Christians are indeed sinners, but they prefer to think of themselves as 'honorary' sinners, not real sinners. In other words, the community of believers refuses to identify with the prodigal. That created an asymmetrical hermeneutic: the father still stands for God, the older son for the Jews, but the younger son they assign to Christians who had gone astray but not to themselves. The only prodigals left are Christians who have gone astray. They thus left themselves out of the parable. They thought their role was so secure that they were superior to the parable and beyond its reach.

This shift in understanding coincides with the new role assigned to Jesus in the orthodox epic. The story of Jesus is said to culminate in the cross, and the cross means that Christ died for our sins. Put in other language, Christ assuaged the Father's demand for satisfaction, something the old temple cult could not achieve since sacrifices had to be repeated on a regular basis. From the perspective of the parables, on the other hand, the death of Jesus underscores his absolute integrity, his utter devotion to trust in the Father. Jesus becomes the victim of his own vision: he asks nothing for himself, he claims no exemptions, he sets out for the wilderness with nothing but confidence that God will provide. That is the valid meaning of the cross.

In God's domain, everyone must trust for himself or herself. There is no such thing as vicarious trust. The existentialists used to put the point well by saying that no one can take a bath for you. In God's domain, nobody can have your trust for you. There are no surrogates. There are no external redeemers. Thus the orthodox Christian epic is a corruption of the plot of the parable. However, the cross is an appropriate symbol for the Christian mode of existence, if by the cross we understand that we are all pilgrims embarked on an exodus that is undergirded by nothing other than trust.

The New community of faith

The domain of God is the result of the deconstruction of the old world and the fabrication of the new. That community will be characterized by four things.

The alternative reality that is God's domain cannot be identified by signs or portents. Its presence will not be writ large on the canvas of the universe; there are no warrants for its claims. There are no authenticating miracles.

The alternative reality is the product of trust. We cannot demonstrate that it is present to the satisfaction of those who lack trust. We catch sight of it and then act on the certainty that it is so.

The alternative reality is to be celebrated. It is both a death and rebirth. It is both a wake and a christening. We simultaneously say goodby to the old and hello to the new. Properly understood, that is what baptism is all about: passing through the watery grave on the way to new life. And the eucharist is truly a celebration: it is breaking bread and drinking a toast in the mythical realm of God.

The alternative reality is the unreachable destination of a perpetual journey. Like Moses, we are not permitted to cross over to the promised land. We can see it in the distance across the Jordan.

We are always pilgrims wandering in the desert. If we think we have arrived, we have only fallen back into the grip of the old. That is the power of "Satan." Satan stands for stagnation. Curiously enough the church has functioned as Satan in holding communities of "faith" captive to the old default world of sin and salvation.

Jesus as strong poet

Jesus may be described as a strong poet. In employing this term, I am borrowing a phrase coined by Harold Bloom in his work, *The Western Canon. The Books and Schools of the Ages.* In assembling a western canon of great literature, Bloom attempts to confront greatness directly and ask what makes an author or a work 'canonical.' The answer he gives is "strangeness, a mode of originality that either cannot be assimilated, or that so assimilates us that we cease to see it as strange." When you read a truly canonical author for the first time, "you encounter an uncanny startlement rather than a fulfillment of expectations."[1]

What have we been doing as biblical critics if not attempting to free Jesus (and Paul) from the constraints of the written discourse that surrounds them? That is what red and black is all about. We have been on a quest for strong poets, for poets who startle us with their vision, their admonitions, and pronouncements. As we began to catch the echoes of their voices, our anxieties grew exponentially, much as Isaiah's did when he approached the throne of God. Then we asked ourselves, why not excavate the tradition to its primeval depths and attempt to isolate the central vision, the heated core of the language used to articulate that vision? We could then wait to see what would happen. To achieve our goal, we of course had to jettison much of the New Testament, material which turns out to be the effacement, a flattening, a leveling of the original genius. We discovered that *canon* when applied to the New Testament means

1. *The Western Canon*, p. 3.

something like the opposite of what the term means to Harold Bloom.

Jesus was a strong poet. A strong poet startles us by opening up the world anew. A strong poet modifies the way we see reality; he or she subverts the inherited symbolic universe. That vocation carries with it certain rather obvious prospects and dangers of which we should be aware.

First of all, subverting the old symbolic universe can get you killed. People do not like to have their inherited, comfortable symbolic worlds undermined. They tend to get angry and vengeful when that happens.

To subvert the old universe you need a new language, one that infringes the old dictionaries and grammars. That language is one not yet spoken. Interpreting the new language requires a new grammar and a new vocabulary.

The new language will consist of metaphors, which, as Nietzsche said, express the desire to be different, to be elsewhere. Those metaphors constitute a new grammar.

The transition from the old language to the new will admit of no more than a glimpse.

The new symbolic universe will at first be a subuniverse with a population of one – the founding sage. If it survives, it will attract others who have caught the glimpse. The new universe will be socially constructed.

The words and acts that form part of the emerging nascent symbolic universe will be hammered back into the received tradition by the devotees of the founding sage. The voice of the strong poet will survive only in traces, if at all. A world like the one Jesus envisioned cannot become a universal worldview. To survive, it has to be flattened, simplified, literalized for the masses.

When that happens, it is time to start over. It is time for a radical transformation and the formation of a new community.

Ask, Seek, Knock

T he basic question for interpreters is whether the complex in Luke 11:9–13//Matt 7:7–11, derived from the Sayings Gospel Q, originally referred to petitions addressed to God, or whether the three assurances had to do with horizontal requests addressed to parents or friends or strangers along the road. Of course, it is possible that a prayer request addressed to God was understood to require the appropriate response from a neighbor or stranger, perhaps even an enemy. It seems entirely unlikely that Jesus had in mind manna dropping from heaven in answer to prayer when he gave those assurances to his followers. He appears to have been a realist.

In exploring this question, it will be helpful to have the complex set out in parallel columns for easy reference. It will also be helpful to divide the complex into four relatively discrete segments. Luke is on the left in accordance with scholarly convention.

Luke 11:9–13	Matt 7:7–11
I	I
[9]So I tell you,	
ask—it'll be given to you;	[7]"Ask—it'll be given to you;
seek—you'll find;	seek—you'll find;
knock—it'll be opened for you.	knock—it'll be opened for you.

II
¹⁰Rest assured:
everyone who asks receives;
everyone who seeks finds;
and for the one who knocks it is
opened.
III
¹¹Which of you fathers would
hand his son a snake when it's
fish he's asking for? ¹²Or a scor-
pion when it's an egg he's asking
for?

IV
¹³So if you, worthless as you
are, know how to give your children good gifts, isn't it much
more likely that the heavenly
Father will give holy spirit to
those who ask him?

II
⁸Rest assured:
everyone who asks receives;
everyone who seeks finds;
and for the one who knocks it is
opened.
III
⁹Who among you would hand
a son a stone when it's bread
he's asking for? ¹⁰Again, who
would hand him a snake when
it's fish he's asking for? Of
course no one would!

IV
¹¹So if you, worthless as you
are, know how to give your children good gifts, isn't it much
more likely that your Father in
the heavens will give good
things to those who ask him?

In reconstructing the history of the tradition, scholars must work backwards from the Greek text of the gospels as they have come down to us. In this case, we have to inquire first about the larger context in which the evangelists have preserved a complex.

In the larger sequence in the Gospel of Luke, the Lord's Prayer (11:2–4) is followed by the story of the friend at midnight (11:5–8), which in turn is followed by the "ask, seek, knock" com-plex. When combined with the segment IV of the complex ("the heavenly Father will give good gifts to those who ask him"), Luke obviously takes the context to be that of prayer addressed to God. The larger context only confirms the theme of segment IV.

The "ask, seek, knock" complex lacks a prayer context in Matthew. It appears to stand on its own, without relation to what precedes and what follows. If Luke has preserved the larger Q-context, why did Matthew not adopt that same context for his gospel? Is it possible that Luke has created a whole sequence of prayer segments out of independent segments of the tradition? To answer that question, we must decide what text the two evangelists had before them in Q, and whether the Q text reflects development from some more original form going back to Jesus.

The close verbal parallels indicate that both Matthew and Luke derived the "ask, seek, knock" complex from the Sayings Gospel Q. Many scholars are inclined to the view that Luke is more faithful to the Q context than was Matthew and accordingly attribute the prayer context to Q. That is because the Lord's Prayer immediately precedes this complex, if we accept Luke's sequence. Matthew has deliberately moved the "ask, seek, knock" segment to a different location in his gospel, without any apparent reason for doing so. It seems more likely that Luke has built up a prayer context out of disparate elements than that Matthew ignored that context if it had already been assembled in Q.

We must now examine the "ask, seek, knock" sequence by itself.

From this point on the decisions get more difficult. If we assume that this complex, or its predecessor, traveled orally for some months or years before it was written down, what would its oral form likely to have been? It is unlikely that the four-part complex set out above in parallel columns was transmitted orally. It is a bit too complicated and suggests that the compilation in its Q form betrays scribal (written) activity.

The catchy three-line opening assurance, on the other hand, probably represents the core of the tradition. The triplet ask, seek, knock reflects an oral preference for threes and for repetition. It is possible that the second set of assurances, which merely repeat the first, shorter set, could have trailed along in the oral world. It is the third segment that conveys the first hint that some scribe has assembled materials in written form that did not come directly from oral tradition. In that segment, the metaphor switches to how fathers may be expected to respond to requests from sons. That is the first hint of a possible prayer setting. After all, father is the primary metaphor for God. On the other hand, it is also possible that how fathers respond to children was taken as the paradigm for the response of neighbors and even strangers.

The prayer interpretation does not become explicit until we come to the fourth segment. And that segment can readily be understood as an appended generalization suggested by the father metaphor in the third segment. In other words, as the tradition sought to establish the meaning of the tripartite set of assurances in segment I, it selected the father metaphor as the appropriate metaphor for the behavior of those to whom requests for help are addressed. And the requests in question have to do with food. We may take that as the first attempt to specify the original context. Once the father metaphor is attached to the complex, whether in oral or written form, that addition prompted the further generalization about God as the reliable father responding to the requests of children. That addition probably came with its reduction to writing in Q.

It seems probable that only the first triplet can be attributed to Jesus with any confidence. This probability becomes even greater if we are entitled to read it horizontally as a part of his experience on the road in Galilee. As wandering teachers, he and his disciples would have required regular handouts from people they met along the way. That prospect apparently did not trouble him. His unbridled confidence in fellow human beings seems to have characterized his life. Even the enemy is viewed as potentially a savior in the parable of the Samaritan. The focus on the realities of the laws of hospitality in the ancient world comports with his focus on the everyday world around him. Requests addressed to God for food and drink seem abstract and unreal by comparison. Nevertheless, the behavior of neighbors and strangers is brought under the umbrella of God's rule, in the same way and with the same assurance that the poor are designated the primary citizens of the divine domain.

We thus have three stages of the tradition:

1. The threefold assurance originated with Jesus
2. With the addition of segments III and IV in Q, the prayer context emerged
3. Luke enhanced that context by creating a larger prayer sequence of disparate materials

The Samaritan

T he Parable of the Good Samaritan is commonly understood as an example story. Everyone knows what it "means," including the author of the Gospel of Luke, who records it as the answer to the query, "Who is my neighbor?" The story of the Samaritan presumably answers that question: a neighbor is someone who helps another in need. The Samaritan is therefore an example of what it means to be a good neighbor. That is why we call the Samaritan "good," and "Samaritan" has come to be a metaphor for anyone who lends a helping hand.

It is quite possible to read the parable of the Samaritan this way. But I believe Jesus formulated it as a parable, and specifically as a parable of grace. The primary reason for my conviction is that the story itself does not invite the listener to view it as an example of what it means to be a good neighbor.

Every story is so constructed as to invite the reader or listener (we are dealing with oral storytelling and thus with listeners) to view events from a certain perspective. Stories are told from a point of view. Those of us who listen in are turned into observers of events from a vantage point that is dictated by the story itself. The first question we must ask of this miniature story is how the story positions us as auditors.

The parable begins: "This guy was on his way down the road leading from Jerusalem to Jericho when he was set upon by robbers, who stripped his clothes off, beat him up, and ran off, leaving him for dead."

The lead sentence places auditors in the ditch with the Jew who had been mugged and assaulted. We look out on the scene from our battered bodies and empty purses. We silently protest at the treatment. At the same time, we are realists. As auditors we confess: What could we expect? After all, the Jericho road is a dangerous, lonely road that one should not travel alone. We knew that. We were taking unnecessary chances.

The initial perspective of the narrative draws the listener into the story on the side of the victim in the ditch. We shudder because we know the story is true to life.

From our vantage point in the ditch, we observe: "Now by chance a priest was going down that road; when he caught sight of the victim, he went out of his way to avoid him."

The peasants in Jesus' audience snicker at the stereotype: We all know, don't we, that priests are callous and indifferent to the needs of others? They are concerned exclusively for their own well being. This priest was probably on his way to a holiday in the Jordan Valley, perhaps at Jericho, to enjoy the refreshing waters of the Jericho spring and the mild temperatures. From our standpoint, the story continues to run true to life: What more can we expect from rich and powerful priests?

If there were clergy in the audience, they would have taken a defensive posture. They would have reasoned to themselves: "We must consider the possibility of ritual defilement by coming into contact with a corpse." (The fellow may be dead.) Or, "we have to worry about the risk of contact with blood," which would also have meant defilement and a series of rituals to reestablish purity. One cannot be too careful as a servant of God in the temple!

The audience has now taken up sides. The predominant opinion is that the priests are scoundrels. A minority opinion is that ritual defilement was a serious matter and should not be treated lightly.

The story continues: "In the same way, when a Levite came to the place, he took one look at the victim and crossed the road to avoid him."

We all know the Levites are also servants of the temple cult. They are the musicians and the stewards who look after endless details connected with the daily sacrifices. Like the priests, they too must preserve ritual purity if they are to be allowed to perform their sacred duties.

The division in the audience widens. The common people, who probably regarded the temple cult with suspicion anyway, are now convinced their suspicions are justified. The priests and Levites are interested only in protecting their interests. And the temple with its enormous wealth – the temple was the equivalent of a national bank – and its political power – the Sadducees were mostly wealthy priests and community leaders who were friends of the Romans – was regarded with disdain by the many poor. Those with clerical sympathies have now stiffened and begin to resent the picture being painted of them.

The two groups have meanwhile forgotten the victim in the ditch in their contrasting responses to the appearance of the priest and Levite, both of whom elect to ignore the poor fellow lying prostrate before them; instead, they have focused on each other. Now they are about to receive a jolt that will cause them to revert to their original perspective – that of the victim.

The role of the Samaritan is treated with greater detail than that of either the priest or the Levite. It takes up more than half of the brief story. It is as though Jesus is deliberately prolonging this part of the story, perhaps with a touch of irony, even sarcasm.

Here a digression is necessary in order to provide a bit of historical background.

The Samaritans, although near relatives of the Judeans, were regarded as mortal enemies. They occupied the land separating Galilee to the north from Judea to the south. The Samaritans were a strict Torah-observing sect who claimed to preserve the true heritage of the Pentateuch – the first five books of the Bible. They revered the same books as the Jerusalem cult but disagreed on everything else. The Samaritans had built their temple atop Mt. Gerizim, a few miles north of Jerusalem. They regarded the Judeans to the south as heretics who had strayed from their original worship on Mt. Gerizim by building a temple in Jerusalem. John Hyrcanus, a Judean ruler, destroyed the Samaritan temple in 128 B.C.E. That only deepened the hostility between the two cousins.

So fierce was the rivalry between them that Jewish pilgrims from Galilee often crossed the Jordan to the east to make the journey south via Jericho in order to avoid contact with the Samaritans, even though the route though Samaria was much shorter. The Galileans who sometimes ventured across that alien terrain were regularly refused hospitality and occasionally met with violence.

This history is absolutely essential to understand what Jesus was doing in introducing the Samaritan into his story.

To return now to the parable.

Jesus' listeners are not prepared for the appearance of the Samaritan. There is no more head nodding among the poor peasants or the friends of the priests and Levites. A group so recently divided is suddenly reunited at the appearance of the Samaritan. And, would you believe it, Jesus has this traveler, perhaps a merchant, stop and help the poor victim in the ditch. He treats him with olive oil and wine, the equivalent of hydrogen peroxide and a gauze bandage, and sets him on his donkey. He takes him to the inn, where he offers to pay the bill for additional care. It is as though a modern Israeli were to be treated in this unbelievable fashion by a member of the PLO or the Hezbollah. We have been abruptly introduced into the surprises associated with God's domain, for that is what this parable is intended to portray.

The verisimilitude, the plausibility of the tale collapses in this fairy tale ending. The story has made the victim in the ditch unable to resist, to refuse aid from a hated Samaritan. And the Samaritan is represented as acting against type in offering to assist. And the listeners are simply incensed that Jesus would award the hero's role to the Samaritan.

Think now of the aphorisms of Jesus and ask yourself which of his sayings goes with this parable. One thinks immediately of "love your enemies." But while that admonition comports with the actions of the Samaritan, it does not pertain to the victim.

Remember, the initial perspective of the story, the point of view we were obliged to adopt as our own, was that of the fellow who had been robbed and left for dead. From our point of view, the injunction would have to be turned around: "Let your enemies love you."

In either form, the admonition is unthinkable in a tribal honor/shame culture. Love was reserved for tribal members. Hate was the order of the day for aliens and members of other tribes. The story simply subverts the lived world of the peasants in Jesus' audience. Yet someone, or some few, apparently caught sight of what he was talking about, saw how revolutionary it was, and decided to lay claim to the new world of God's domain in exchange for the old universe of tribal enmity and frustrated hopes.

Scholars are sometimes asked why Jesus was killed. Very complex political, social, and theological answers have been given to this question, any or all of which have some degree of validity. But a simple rejoinder may be quite adequate: The parable of the Samaritan could easily have gotten Jesus killed.

An enterprising theologian could perhaps elicit a few generalizations from this story. These seem fitting:

In God's domain,

Help comes from the quarter from which we don't want it.
Help comes from the quarter from which we least expect it.
Help always comes as a surprise.
Help is another name for grace – the grace of the Samaritan who was scandalously generous.[17]

17. My thanks to Bill Reed for suggesting the wording of the last line.

Database

The following is a database of the sayings that comprise the vision of Jesus described in the pages of this book. In the case where a saying survived in multiple versions, the specific version used as the basis of the commentary is given in bold.

Able-bodied & Sick
Sources: Mark, Gospel
Fragment 1224, common lore
Mark 2:16–17//GosFr 1224
5:2//Matt 9:11–12//
Luke 5:30–31, p. 37

Anxieties
Source: Q
Matt 6:25//Thom 36:1//
Luke 12:22–23, p. 29

Ask, Seek, Knock.
Source: Q
Luke 11:9–10//Matt 7:7–8//
Thom 94:1–2//Thom 2:1–4,
p. 30

Award to the Hungry
Source: Q
Luke 6:21a//Matt 5:6//Thom
69:2, p. 37

Award to the Poor
Source: Q
Luke 6:20//Thomas 54//Matt
5:3, pp. 19, 117

Award to the Tearful
Source: Q
Luke 6:21b//Matt 5:4, p. 37

Before the Judge
Source: Q
Luke 12:58–59//Matt 5:25–26,
p. 95

Bread for the Day
Source: Q
Matt 6:11//Luke 11:3, p. 30

Care for the Dead
Source: Q
Luke 9:60//Matt 8:22, p. 87

Friend at Midnight
Source: Luke
Luke 11:5–8, p. 30

Give to Beggars
Source: Q
Matt 5:42a//Luke 6:30a, pp. 95, 117

God & Birds
Source Q
Matt 6:26//Luke 12:24, pp. 29, 79

God & Crows
Source: Q
Luke 12:24//Matt 6:26, p. 30

God & Grass
Source Q
Luke 12:28//Matt 6:30, pp. 29, 79

God & Hair
Source Q
Luke 12:7a//Matt 10:30, pp. 30, 80

God & Lilies
Source Q
Matt 6:28–29//Luke 12:27//Thom 36:2, pp. 29, 79

God & Sparrows (1)
Source: Q
Luke 12:6//Matt 10:29, pp. 29, 79

God & Sparrows (2)
Source Q
Matt 10:29//Luke 12:6, pp. 29, 79

Hating One's Family (1)
Sources: Q, Thomas
Luke 14:26–27//Thom 55:1–2//
Matt 10:37–38//Thom 101:1–3, p. 71

Hating One's Family (2)
Sources: Q, Thomas
Thom 55:1–2//Luke 14:26–27//
Matt 10:37–38//Thom 101:1–3, p. 71

House Divided
Sources: Q, Mark
Luke 11:17–18//Matt 12:25–26//
Mark 3:23–26, p. 103

In League with Satan
Sources: Mark, Q
Mark 3:20–26//Matt 12:22–28//
Luke 11:14–20, pp. 103–104

Inside & Outside
Sources: Thomas, Q
Thom 89:1–2//Matt 23:25–26//
Luke 11:39–41, p. 43

Jesus and John the Baptist
Source: Q
Luke 7:32–34, p. 37

Leaven
Sources: Q, Thomas
Luke 13:20–21//Matt 143:33//
Thom 96:1–2, pp. 81, 91

Left & Right Hands
Sources: Matthew, Thomas
Matt 6:3//Thom 62:2, p. 118

Lend without Return
Sources: Thomas, Q
Thom 95:1–2//Matt 5:42b//Luke
6:34–35c, pp. 95, 117

Lepers
Sources: Mark, Egerton Gospel
Mark 1:40–45//Matt 8:1–4//Luke
5:12–16//GEger 2:1–4, pp. 43–44

Liberal Love
Source: Q
Matt 5:48, p. 109

Lords of the Sabbath
Source: Mark
Mark 2:27–28//Matt 12:8//Luke
6:5, p. 126

Lost Coin
Source: Luke
Luke 15:8–9, pp. 35, 117

Lost Sheep
Sources: Q, Thomas
Luke 15:4–6//Matt
18:12–13//Thom 107:1–3, pp.
35–36, 81, 117–18

Love of Enemies
Source: Q
Luke 6:27–28//Matt 5:44//Luke
6:35a, p. 57

Love Your Enemies
Source: Q
Luke 6:35a//Matt 5:44b//Luke
6:27b, p. 110

Mustard Seed
Sources: Thomas, Mark, Q
Thom 20:2–4//Mark 4:30–32//
Luke 13:18–19//Matt 13:31–32,
pp. 80, 91

The Narrow Door
Sources: Q, Thomas
Luke 13:24//Matt 7:13–14, p. 147

Needle's Eye
Source: Mark
Matt 19:24//Luke 18:25//Mark
10:25, pp. 19, 81

No Merit in Love
Source: Q
Matt 5:46//Luke 6:32, pp. 57, 109

Not What Goes In
Sources: Mark, Thomas
Mark 7:15//Thom 14:5//Matt
15:11, p. 118

Number One as Servant
Source: Mark
Mark 9:35; cf. Matt 23:11//Luke
9:48b, p. 87

The Other Cheek
Source: Q
Matt 5:39//Luke 6:29a, p. 95

Pharisee & Toll Collector
Source: Luke
Luke 18:10–14a, p. 119

Powerful Man
Sources: Mark, Q, Thomas
Matt 12:29//Mark 3:27//Thom
35:1–2//Luke 11:21–22, p. 104

Precious Pearl
Sources: Thomas, Matthew
Thom 76:1–2//Matt 13:45–46,
p. 81

Prodigal Son
Source: Luke
Luke 15:11–32, pp. 36–37

Prophets without Honor; Doctors without Cures
Sources: Thomas, Mark, John
Thom 31:1–2//Luke 4:24//John
4:44//Matt 13:57//Mark 6:4, p. 43

Rich Farmer
Sources: Thomas, Luke
Thom 63:1–3//Luke 12:16–20,
p. 20

Rules for the Road (1)
Sources: Thomas, Q
Thom 14:4a//Luke 10:8, p. 126

Rules for the Road (2)
Source: Q
Luke 10:7a, p. 126

The Samaritan
Source: Luke
Luke 10:30–35, pp. 57, 125

Satan's Fall
Source: Luke
Luke 10:18, p. 103

Saving One's Life
Sources: Q, Mark, John
Luke 17:33//Matt 16:25//Matt
10:39//Luke 9:24//John 12:25//
Mark 8:35, pp. 87, 119

Scholars' Privileges
Sources: Q, Mark
Luke 20:45–47//Mark 12:38–39//
Matt 23:5–7//Luke 11:43, pp, 119,
126

Second Mile
Source: Q
Matt 5:41, p. 95

Seed & Harvest
Source: Mark
Mark 4:26–29//Thom 21:9, p. 80

Shrewd Manager
Source: Luke
Luke 16:1–8a, p. 88

Sliver & Timber
Sources: Thomas, Q
Thom 26:1–2//Matt 7:3–5//Luke
6:41–42, p. 118

Sly as a Snake
Sources: Matthew, Thomas
Matt 10:16//Thom 39:3, p. 82

The Sower
Source: Mark
Mark 4:3–8//Matt 13:3–8//Thom
9:1–5//Luke 8:5–8a, p. 80

Sun & Rain
Source: Q
Matt 5:45b, pp. 57, 80, 109

The Temple Incident
Source: Mark
Mark 11:15–17//Matt 21:12–13//
Luke 19:45–46//John 2:13–16,
p. 125

Reading Suggestions & References

For those who wish to pursue certain themes, or sample other opinion, or consult sources on which the author may have drawn, the following reading suggestions may be of interest.

Bibliography

Hans Dieter Betz, *The Sermon on the Mount.* Edited Adela Yarbro Collins. Hermeneia – A Historical Critical Commentary on the Bible. Minneapolis: Fortress Press, 1995.

Marcus Borg, *Meeting Jesus Again for the First Time.* HarperSanFrancisco, 1994.

James Carroll, *Constantine's Sword. The Church and the Jews.* Boston: Houghton Mifflin Company, 2001.

John Dominic Crossan, *The Birth of Christianity.* HarperSanFrancisco, 1998.

John Dominic Crossan, *The Dark Interval. Towards A Theology of Story.* Santa Rosa, CA: Polebridge Press, 1988.

John Dominic Crossan, *The Historical Jesus. The Life of a Mediterranean Jewish Peasant.* HarperSanFrancisco, 1991.

John Dominic Crossan, *In Fragments. The Aphorisms of Jesus.* San Francisco: Harper & Row, Publishers, 1983.

John Dominic Crossan, *Jesus. A Revolutionary Biography.* HarperSanFrancisco, 1994.

William Dever, *The Rise of Ancient Israel.* Edited by Herschel Shanks. Biblical Archaeology Society, 1992.

Joseph A. Fitzmyer, *The Gospel According to Luke,* 2 Vols. The Anchor Bible. New York: Doubleday & Company, Inc., 1981 and 1986.

Robert Funk & The Jesus Seminar. *The Acts of Jesus. The Search for the Authentic Deeds of Jesus.* HarperSanFrancisco, 1998.

Robert W Funk, Roy Hoover and The Jesus Seminar. *The Five Gospels. The Search for the Authentic Words of Jesus.* New York: Macmillan, 1993.

Robert W. Funk, *Honest to Jesus.* HarperSanFrancisco, 1996.

Lloyd Geering, *Christianity without God.* Santa Rosa, CA: Polebridge Press, forthcoming in 2002.

Lloyd Geering, *The World to Come. From Christian Past to Global Future.* Santa Rosa, CA: Polebridge Press, 1999.

John Hick, *The Fifth Dimension. An Exploration of the Spiritual Realm.* Oxford: One World, 1999.

John S. Kloppenborg Verbin, *Excavating Q. The History and Setting of the Sayings Gospel.* Minneapolis: Fortress Press, 2000.

Robert J. Miller, editor, *The Complete Gospels.* Santa Rosa, CA: Polebridge Press, 1992, 1994.

Robert J. Miller, *The Jesus Seminar and Its Critics.* Santa Rosa, CA: Polebridge Press, 1999.

Stephen J. Patterson, *The God of Jesus.* Harrisburg, PA: Trinity Press International, 1998.

Stephen J. Patterson, *The Gospel of Thomas and Jesus.* Santa Rosa, CA: Polebridge Press, 1993.

Norman Perrin, *Rediscovering the Teaching of Jesus.* New York: Harper & Row, Publishers, 1976.

Ronald A. Piper, *Wisdom in the Q-Tradition. The Aphoristic Teaching of Jesus.* Cambridge: Cambridge University Press, 1989.

Anne Primavesi, *Sacred Gaia. Holistic Theology and Earth System Science.* London and New York: Routledge, 2000.

Bernard Brandon Scott, *Hear Then the Parable. A Commentary on the Parables of Jesus.* Minneapolis: Fortress Press, 1989.

Bernard Brandon Scott, *Re-Imagine the World. An Introduction to the Parables of Jesus.* Santa Rosa, CA: Polebridge Press, 2001.

John Shelby Spong, *Why Christianity Must Change or Die.* HarperSanFrancisco, 1998.

Paul Veyne, editor. *A History of Private Life.* Cambridge, MA: Harvard University Press, 1987.

Walter Wink, *Engaging the Powers.* Minneapolis: Fortress Press, 1992.

Reading Suggestions & References

Introduction: Voice Print
    Social Context and Rhetoric of Q:
        Kloppenborg Verbin, *Excavating Q,* 198–206.
    Jesus as Wisdom Teacher:
        Geering, *Christianity without God,* chapter 9.

1. The Invisible Realm
The Poor:
> Crossan, *The Historical Jesus,* 270–74.
> Crossan, *Jesus,* 61–62.

Kingdom and Riches:
> Crossan, *The Historical Jesus,* 274–76.

Nobodies:
> Crossan, *Jesus,* 64–66.

Thom 113:1–4//Luke 17:20–21:
> Patterson, *Thomas and Jesus,* 71–72; 208–9; 224.
> Fitzmyer, *Luke,* Vol. II, 1161–62.
> Perrin, *Rediscovering,* 68–77.

2. A Trust Ethic
Ask, Seek, Knock:
> Crossan, *In Fragments,* 95–104.
> Fitzmyer, *Luke,* Vol. II, 913–16.
> Betz, *Sermon on the Mount,* 500–508.
> Ronald Piper, *Wisdom,* 15–24.

Friend at Midnight:
> Fitzmyer, *Luke,* Vol. II, 909–13.

3. Celebration
> Funk, *Honest to Jesus,* 146–47; 208–9.

4. Outsiders & Outcasts
Inside/outside:
> Robert J. Miller, "The Inside is (Not) the Outside," *Forum* 5, 1 (March 1989), 92–105.

Crossan, *In Fragments,* 250.

Children:
> Veyne, *A History of Private Life,* 9–31.
> Crossan, *Revolutionary Biography,* 60–66.
> Crossan, *The Historical Jesus,* 266–69; 274–76.

Toll collectors:
> Betz, *Sermon on the Mount,* 318–19.
> Fitzmyer, *Luke,* Vol. I, 465; 591–92; Vol. II, 1218–27.

5. Transcending Tribalism
Love your enemies:
> Betz, *Sermon on the Mount,* 301–28.
> Kloppenborg Verbin, *Excavating Q,* 411–12.

Samaritan
> Funk, *Honest to Jesus,* 170–80.

Scott, *Hear Then the Parable,* 189–202.
Scott, *Reimagine the World,* 55–64.

6. Kinship
Veyne, *A History of Private Life,* 9–31.
Patterson, *Thomas and Jesus,* 44–45, 230–31.

Four-room House:
Larry Stager, "Archaeology of the Family," *Biblical Archaeology Review* (1989) 50–64.
Dever, *The Rise of Ancient Israel,* 38–40.

7. Flora & Fauna
Primavesi, *Sacred Gaia,* 21–23, 37–49, 160, and passim.
Geering, *The World to Come,* 123–34.

8. Values Are Counterintuitive
Crossan, *Dark Interval*

9. New Symbols Parody the Old
Scott, *Hear Then the Parable,* 321–29.
Scott, *Reimagine the World,* 119–40.

10. Subverting the System
Wink, *Engaging the Powers,* 175–93.
Betz, *Sermon on the Mount,* 274–93.
Crossan, *The Birth of Christianity,* 393–95

13. Humor & Humility
Funk, *Honest to Jesus,* 146–47; 208–9.

14. End of Brokered Religion
Borg, *Meeting Jesus Again,* 127–33, 140 n. 25.
Spong, *Why Christianity Must Change,* 83–99.

16. God's Domain as Mythic Destination
Spong, *How Christianity Must Change,* 22–42.

17. The Cross as Symbol of Integrity
Carroll, *Constantine's Sword*
Hick, *Fifth Dimension,* 237.

Index of Scripture

Items in bold in this index are part of the database. See appendix 3.

183

The Jesus Seminar is a project of the Westar Institute, a private, non-profit institute devoted to improving biblical and religious literacy by making the scholarship of religion available and accessible to the general public. As part of its literacy program, the Institute sponsors semi-annual seminar meetings, "Jesus Seminar on the Road" programs, and publications in the field of religion.

Membership in the Westar Institute is open to professional scholars as Fellows and to all others as Associates. Membership benefits include a subscription to the magazine of the Westar Institute – The Fourth R – and notices of national and regional meetings of the Jesus Seminar.

To learn more about the Westar Institute, please contact:

The Westar Institute
P.O. Box 6144
Santa Rosa, California 95406
707 523-1323
707 523-1350 fax
members@westarinstitute.org
www.WestarInstitute.org